EYEGLASSES

EYEGLASSES

Translated from the French by Jonathan Sly
Copyediting: Kate Lancaster
Typesetting: Claude-Olivier Four
Proofreading: Linda Gardiner
Color separation by Chesteroc Graphics
Printed in France by I.M.E.

Originally published as La Folie des Lunettes © Editions Flammarion 2003
English-language edition © Editions Flammarion 2004

Editions Flammarion
26, rue Racine
75006 Paris

www.editions.flammarion.com

04 05 06 3 2 1

FC0437-04-III
ISBN: 2-0803-0437-2
Dépôt legal: 03/2004

Collectible
EYEGLASSES

Frédérique Crestin-Billet

Flammarion

By the same author

Collectible Playing Cards
Éditions Flammarion
(2002)

Collectible Corkscrews
Éditions Flammarion
(2001)

When I was a child, in the sixties, I lived in Morez, a gray little town clutching the side of the Jura Mountains, near where France borders Switzerland. Morez had many workshops, all bustling with activity whenever we went past on our way to school.

On Thursdays, my cousins, sisters, and I would go to my grandmother's house. Opposite was the famous Cébé eyeglasses factory, owned by one of my uncles. It was here, in the backyard, that we played with jump ropes made from the blue and white elastic straps that were used for ski goggles worn by the likes of Killy, Lacroix, and Périllat.

CONTENTS

Introduction

I grew up at the heart of the French eyeglasses industry. Whenever a member of my family needed a pair of glasses, all they had to do was visit the workshop. In no time at all, they would re-emerge, their nose crowned with a fine new pair of frames, selected from among the hundred of batches of stock waiting to be dispatched. For many of us, eyeglasses seemed to be part of the furniture and ceased to have any special meaning. Indeed, it was not until recently that I realized how little written praise eyeglasses have enjoyed for the vital job they do.

INTRODUCTION

The birth and development of the eyeglasses industry in the east of France can be attributed to one man: Pierre-Hyacinthe Caseaux. However, as to who invented eyeglasses nobody can quite agree.

The Romans could have been first on the block. Not because they conceived of eyeglasses per se, but because they discovered magnifying lenses. Extensive excavation of ancient Roman sites has unearthed convex glass or quartz crystal lenses. These lenses were often punctured in the middle and are barely transparent. Archeologists were swift to conclude that Roman lenses were simply decorations to be affixed to weapons, belts or clothing. The Emperor Nero (37–68 C.E.), meanwhile, would view gladiatorial bouts through an emerald mounted on a ring, leading some

Two eggcup-like eyebaths. Before the invention of eyeglasses, lotions, eyewashes, and balms were the only available ways of treating eyesight problems.

historians to deduce—perhaps too hastily—that the cruel emperor used the precious stone as a magnifying glass or monocle. The Roman writer and historian, Pliny the Elder (23–79 C.E.), is responsible for the anecdote, and commentators often overlook the lines preceding his oft-quoted extract, which state: "Indeed, no stone has a color that is more delightful to the eye. Sculptors of stone or crystal would restore and refresh their sight by gazing upon an emerald. Nero himself would hold an emerald to his eye to watch the gladiator games." Pliny's point is crystal clear— the emerald was prized for its curative, not magnifying, power. Yet, while we know that the Romans were aware of the magnifying power of a bowl of water, no practical application seems to have been made of the phenomenon.

Another possible pioneer was the Arab scholar, Al-Hazen (965–1039). In his book *Opticae Thesaurus* (a treatise on optics), he was the first

to offer a scientific description of the magnifying potentials
of lenses of different shapes, but his work does not
mention their possible utility for reading.
Two and a half centuries later, however,
references to reading aids appear in German literature.
Conrad of Würzburg's (1230–1287) songs speak
of "reading stones"—flat-convex lenses (with one
flat surface and the other convex) that the reader
would shunt slowly across the surface being read.
"Reading stones" did not last long because shortly
afterwards the magnifying glass was discovered,
made of a convergent or double-convex lens
(in other words a lens with two convex sides)
set in a frame and held by a handle.
Its actual inventor, however, is unknown.

*Since its invention, the form of the magnifying glass has not really changed,
except that it has become "binocular," affording magnified stereoscopic vision.
We still use magnifying glasses today; certain professions, such as photographers
and clockmakers, have their own specialized versions.*

...ESHWAR, ville de l'Empire angl... ...de, État vassal d'Indore, sur le Nerb... ...très ancienne, aux sanctuaires vénérés.

MAHEUTRE [ma-eutr'] n. m. (de *mahut*). Manche qui couvrait le bras depuis l'épaule jusqu'au coude, du temps de Louis XI. || Coussin avec lequel on rembourrait cette manche. (On trouve aussi MAHEUTRE, et MAHOITRE.)

— *Par extens.* Soldat dont le vêtement portait des maheutres. || En 1590, Soldat dont la maheutrerie royaliste : *Un carabin ma-* HEUTRE du parti du roi de Navarre. (Naudé.)

— *Par anal.* Bandit, assassin, à cause des excès commis par les maheutres :

C'est un *maheutre* et un frelu,
Pire qu'un Turc ou Mamelu.
(*Catholicon.*)

MAHIEU (Thomas), célèbre bibliophile français, longtemps appelé *Maioli* d'après la devise portée sur la reliure des livres lui ayant appartenu. Il signait encore... ...comme trésorier de France et général de ses f... ...large et généralité de la Langue d'oïl. Les... ...histoire de la reliure.

A. Maheutre (XVe s.

Roger Bacon, nicknamed Doctor Mirabilis *(Professor Marvel).*

At about the same time as Conrad of Würzburg's "reading stones" appeared, in 1267, the Franciscan monk, Roger Bacon (1214–1294) produced his *Opus Majus*. The monk was one of the greatest scholars of the thirteenth century; he had an inventive mind and passionately defended experimental science. Somewhat unwisely, however, he published the results of all of his experiments, and was charged with commerce with the devil. Bacon was imprisoned several times, despite the protection he received from Pope Clement IV. In the *Opus Majus*, he wrote: "We can so shape transparent bodies, and arrange them in such a way with respect to our sight and objects of vision, that the rays will be refracted and bent in any direction that we desire, and under any angle we wish we shall see the object near or at a distance." And by so saying, Bacon proved that not only did he know about lenses and what they could do, but that he also had access to such objects.

Dual-lensed, single-framed eyeglasses first appeared not in England or France, however, but in Italy. The difficulty in identifying *the* inventor of such glasses is that there are several names associated with their emergence. The first is Alessandro da Spina, a Dominican monk who died in 1313. Da Spina is cited in the chronicles of the Pisan convent of Saint Catherine as a good and generous man who was naturally gifted with his hands. The chronicles speak of his ability to reproduce objects faithfully, including articles of which he had only heard but never seen. Having been told of the invention of eyeglasses, he produced pairs himself and, charitably,

Nineteenth century ex-votos that were hung in churches to offer thanks to God for curing eye afflictions.

shared his skill with others. Although it does not seem that Brother da Spina was the actual inventor of eyeglasses, he was nevertheless an important figure who encouraged their propagation on a small scale. That eyeglasses were becoming more widely used was confirmed in a sermon by another Dominican, Brother Giordano da Rivalta, who, in 1305, declared: "It is not yet twenty years since the art of making spectacles, one of the most useful arts on earth, was discovered." In the same year, Bernard Gordon, professor at the university medical school in Montpellier, France, in his *Lilium Medicinae* drew attention to an eyewash that he said was so effective it enabled old men to read *sine ocularibus* (without glasses). This is proof enough that eyeglasses must already have existed from the 1280s onwards.

So who did invent them? One name that has been put forward is that of Salvino d'Armato, a Florentine gentleman. In 1684, Leopoldo del Migliore, author of an illustrated work on Florence, claims to have read the following inscription

Sample case with adjustable glasses and an assortment of additional lenses. When eyeglasses were first invented, they could only treat problems of presbyopia, where vision deteriorates with age. Other eyesight problems could not be treated until later.

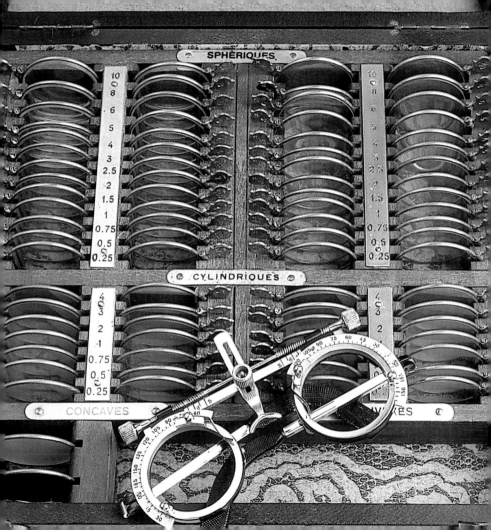

in the Santa Maria Maggiore church: "Here lies Salvino d'Armato, of the Armati of Florence, inventor of eyeglasses. May God pardon his sins. A.D. 1317." However, del Migliore's work, written in the seventeenth century, is the first instance of d'Armato being cited as the rightful inventor. Furthermore, nineteenth century archeologists cast a doubt on the authenticity of the tombstone, and today this tombstone cannot be found.

In the haze of mystery surrounding the identity of the inventor of eyeglasses, one undisputed fact stands out—in 1268 Roger Bacon's manuscript had already arrived in Italy and was in the hands of the Church. Bacon had sent the work to his protector Pope Clement IV, who died the same year. His successor was Pope John XXI, who prior to becoming Pope was a doctor, theologian, and philosopher by the name of Petrus Hispanus. He had studied at the University of Paris between 1240 and 1247, while Roger Bacon was also there. It is therefore not unreasonable to believe that his attention might already have been drawn to Bacon's work, either when he was Petrus Hispanus, doctor of medicine at the University of Siena, or, later, as Pope John XXI. In either role, he would have been in a position to encourage the manufacture of the first eyeglasses.

The writer Marcel Achard in 1959, before his election to the elite scholarly institution, the Académie française. Legend has it that apart from his talent and sense of humor, his "kindly myopic expression framed behind a pair of solid lenses" helped him beat out other candidates.

When the new optical aids arrived in England, they were simply called "glasses" or "spectacles." Today, collectors refer to them as "nose-spectacles," to distinguish them from "spectacles," a word reserved for the thin wire-framed variety with side arms. The corrective lenses of "nose-spectacles" were initially made of rock crystal and beryl, a mineral related to emeralds and aquamarine that also has a colorless variety. The lenses were mounted in heavy frames of wood or horn, each affixed to

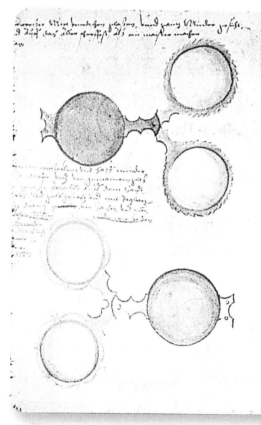

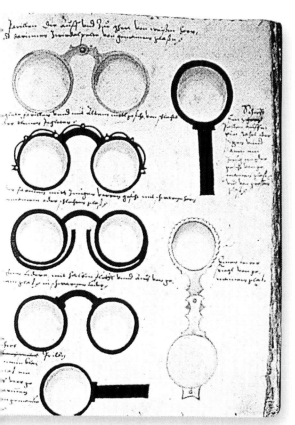

This extraordinary double page spread comes from the first known eyeglasses catalogue. It was produced in Ratisbon, Germany, and dates from around 1600. The idea to use concave lenses to treat myopia, where the image is formed in front of the retina rather than on it, first emerged at the end of the fifteenth century. It was not until Kepler, in the seventeenth century, that the principle of shortsightedness was understood. And it was not until two hundred years later that James Ware differentiated between myopia and hypermetropia, or farsightedness, where the image is formed behind the retina, instead of on it.

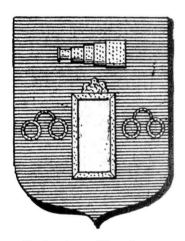

The bearings of the mirror and eyeglass makers' guild, circa 1550: a silver mirror, with a gold frame; two pairs of gold-rimmed glasses, capped with a gold telescope, all on a sky-blue background.

a rod and joined by a nail. Monks in particular wore nose-spectacles, as they were the most literate of the population. In Murano, Italy, the manufacture of convex eyeglasses was regulated from 1300 onwards. The Venetian government imposed punishments on glassmakers who would cut inferior "rounds of glass for glasses for reading". In France, eyeglass manufacture and distribution appeared in the fifteenth century. In Germany, Gutenberg had recently invented the printing press, the Renaissance was flourishing across Europe, and reading was becoming a more widespread activity.

The status of eyeglass makers evolved slowly. In 1465, eyeglass makers were among guildsmen parading before the French king Louis XI, and they marched under the same banner as tapestry-makers and notions sellers.

Almost a century later, they were grouped with mirror cutters, before finally forming a corporation of mirror cutters, eyeglass makers, and fancy goods dealers. In the seventeenth century, they set up stalls along the banks of the Seine, in particular on the quai de l'Horloge. But it was only in 1720 that a distinction was made between artisan eyeglass makers and master opticians, who more specifically produced optical instruments for astronomy and scholarly research.

Late eighteenth century peddler in Meissen porcelain. A peddler's inventory would have included eyeglasses as well as belt buckles, fans, and other assorted objects.

Stalls aside, it was peddlers who were largely responsible for the spread of eyeglasses around Europe. It is worth remembering that, in this period, lenses were sold arbitrarily; the purchase of eyeglasses was governed by no medical considerations.

Broken spectacles and their shagreen case, dating from the eighteenth century. This pair is part of the famous Essilor-Pierre Marly collection, models of which feature extensively in the pages that follow. There is a list of pieces from the collection on page 370.

Facing page: Engraving representing a peddler trying to persuade a gentleman as to the utility of eyeglasses.

While spectacles appeared at the end of the thirteenth century, it took five hundred years before anyone had the idea to attach side arms or sidepieces. Side arms were initially short and generally had ring tips that pressed against the temples (an example appears on page 59). They gradually became longer in the second half of the eighteenth century, to an almost exaggerated extent. Subsequently, a number of mechanisms to slide, fold or adjust them were introduced.

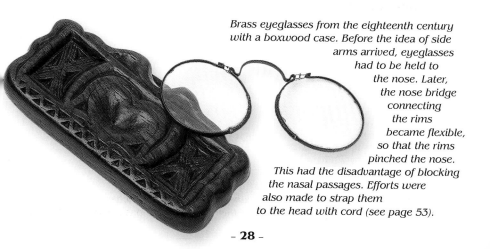

Brass eyeglasses from the eighteenth century with a boxwood case. Before the idea of side arms arrived, eyeglasses had to be held to the nose. Later, the nose bridge connecting the rims became flexible, so that the rims pinched the nose. This had the disadvantage of blocking the nasal passages. Efforts were also made to strap them to the head with cord (see page 53).

owards the end of the eighteenth century, viewing accessories drifted into the world of fashion. The era saw the emergence of scissor-glasses (see pages 66 to 69), as well as finely crafted, handle-fitted monocles, spyglasses, opera-glasses, and lorgnettes in all shapes, sizes, and disguises.

The Incroyables *was a group of rich, young, Royalist socialites during the Directory in France (1795–1799). Their eccentric fashion statement was expressed in their gaudy sense of dress. They would speak without pronouncing the letter "r" and feigned mystery, concealing their facial expressions behind eyeglasses.*

During the nineteenth century, fine metal-wire frames were introduced. Pince-nez also made their appearance and were a great success, despite the way they pinched the nose and hindered breathing, like early spectacles. They remained in fashion until the end of the century. Similarly, a number of lorgnette styles survived, even though side arms that tucked comfortably behind the ears were now a common feature.

A color advertisement produced by a New York City tailor to celebrate New Year 1877. A fashionable gentleman was nobody without a pair of eyeglasses.

I t is at this point that a key player in French eyeglasses history enters the scene. At the end of the eighteenth century, Pierre-Hyacinthe Caseaux (1744–1814) started manufacturing eyeglasses in a small town in the Haut-Jura in eastern France and turned it into the country's eyewear capital. Caseaux was born and raised in the lowlands of the region and, at the age of 33, settled higher up the slopes in a tiny farming hamlet, close to the town of Morez. Nobody quite knows what circumstances drove him to live and work in these mountainous lands that are covered by snow five months in the year. The long harsh winters left Jura farmers a long time to tinker and one of their occupations during this period was to make iron nails, essential in the

Fine metal-wire frames from the end of the nineteenth century, the kind we all find at the back of our great-grandparents' drawers.

construction of the traditional local houses,
which were covered in weather-boards,
small squares of wood that isolated the
north-facing façades. Caseaux's own tale is
told by Michel Bussod and Michel Jean-Prost
in their book on the history of eyeglasses
manufacture in Morez:

"While he was not cultivating the land
and raising cattle, Caseaux would keep
himself busy. He would buy rolls of iron
wire from the hardware store in Morez
and make nails. In the 1790s ...
Pierre-Hyacinthe Caseaux was approaching
his fifties. He was probably presbyopic and
the mechanical work he carried out required
good sight, hence the need for glasses.
It seems he went to the nearest neighboring

*The main road through Morez, rue de la République,
in the 1930s. It is the same road as the N5 highway
that runs from Dijon to Geneva and where most workshops
and factories were once based, as some still are.*

MOREZ *(Jura)* — *Rue de la République*

L. JEANTET

The Morez town crest recalls the age of water wheels. Sawmills and eyeglass manufacturers alike used the hydraulic power of the Bienne River and its tributaries.

large town, Geneva, in Switzerland, and ordered a pair of glasses to correct his vision. Some time later, by accident, his frames broke but the lenses, by a miracle, survived the mishap."

He decided to repair them himself and soon noticed that frames could be copied using iron wire.

Caseaux set to work and offered his prototypes to a jeweler-optician in Geneva. The trial was a success and a first order was made. "Gradually, the news of his early attempts at industry spread to neighboring regions and orders started to come in. Pierre-Hyacinthe Caseaux was overwhelmed by demand. Fortunately his young neighbor and friend, Jean-Baptiste Lamy, was on hand to help him. The partnership lasted a good ten years, producing several hundred frames a year." Caseaux, in his old age, left his workshop to his partner Jean-Baptiste Lamy, who was joined

An eye-catching business card belonging to a small eyeglass manufacturer, of which there are so many in Morez.

by his son, Pierre-Hyacinthe Lamy, the godson of Caseaux. Both had a strong belief in the future of the industry and, in 1819, set up premises in Morez. Many other families soon followed suit, abandoning clock-making which until then had been the town's mainstay. The rest, as they say, is history.

Today, Morez is still the eyewear capital of France. In May 2003, the town inaugurated a new eyewear museum, featuring donations from local families and businesses as well as loans from the prestigious Essilor-Pierre Marly collection (see pages 196 to 198).

The logo of the French Eyeglasses Museum recalls the early eyeglasses of the eighteenth century.

Facing page: While many tasks can be done by machine, the manufacture of eyeglasses requires craftsmen, which is one of the reasons for its shift overseas, notably to China.

Essilor

In 1849, three small steel-frame makers joined together to set up the first eyeglass workers association, the Association fraternelle des ouvriers lunetiers, based at 180, rue Saint-Martin, in Paris. It was a workers' cooperative that quickly prospered, organizing its own production. The network of small workshops it established in Paris soon became insufficient to meet demand. So from the 1860s onward, it set up its first factories in the east of France, in the towns of Ligny-en-Barrois and Saint-Mihiel, and then in Morez, in 1877. It changed its name to the Société des lunetiers or SL, which subsequently became Essel, after the pronunciation of the initials. It expanded its range to cover all manner of optical, topographical, and precision instruments and started selling its products abroad. The business continued to grow and, responding to fashion and demands for new products, introduced Nylor frames on the market, in 1955. The Nylor model had invisible frames and was produced using a totally new method (see page 190). In 1959, Bernard Maitenaz, a young optician (who eventually became the CEO of Essilor from 1980 to 1991), developed the Varilux, the first progressive lens ever made. In 1972, Essel merged with Silor, the industrial sector of the group founded by Georges Lissac, inventor of Amor glasses (see page 187) and the organic-lensed Orma. Since then, Essilor has stopped making frames and concentrated its production on corrective lenses, becoming the world number one in its domain, with a work force of more than twenty-two thousand spread across all five continents. Essilor's history is one of those rare success stories where a cooperative movement has flourished and developed into a major multinational company.

LA MODE
SOUS LE DIRECTOIRE

I

ANTIQUE

eyeglasses

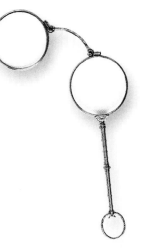

Nose-spectacles, pince-nez, and lorgnettes are all types of eyeglasses that are no longer in use today. This is why I call them "antique" here. Many of the examples in the following pages are either unique pieces or limited-series models. They come from an era where eyeglasses manufacture was not yet an industry but still a craft, or, in certain cases, an art form.

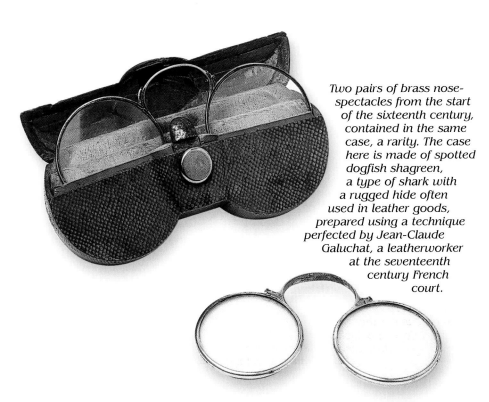

Two pairs of brass nose-spectacles from the start of the sixteenth century, contained in the same case, a rarity. The case here is made of spotted dogfish shagreen, a type of shark with a rugged hide often used in leather goods, prepared using a technique perfected by Jean-Claude Galuchat, a leatherworker at the seventeenth century French court.

A pair of wire-framed nose-spectacles. Note the sections resting on the nose—they are wrapped silk thread. It is most likely that the attractive sculpted-wood case is not the original. Nose-spectacles and their cases are not necessarily birds of a feather.

*As explained
on pages 22 to 24,
the first nose-spectacles were heavy objects made
of wood or horn. The bridge (the part resting on the nose)
was not hinged. In comparison to early models, these eighteenth
century models, with their rustic air, are actually very refined
for their time: their metal bridge is arched to fit the contours
of the nose. Notice the wire clasp sealing the lenses
of the nose-spectacles on the right.*

Until the
French Revolution
when trades' guilds
were abolished, makers of artisan eyeglasses
were not authorized to make cases; these were
the preserve of fancy goods dealers. It is therefore logical that
the two professions were joined within the same corporate body
(see page 25). Note the attractive shape of the case on the left
and the silver wire clasp holding the frames on this pair.

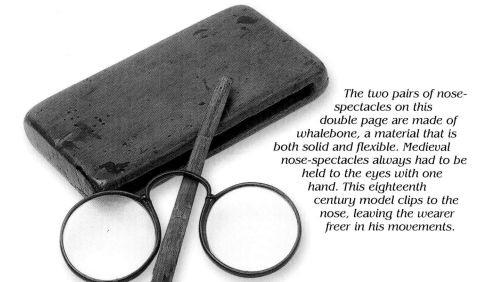

The two pairs of nose-spectacles on this double page are made of whalebone, a material that is both solid and flexible. Medieval nose-spectacles always had to be held to the eyes with one hand. This eighteenth century model clips to the nose, leaving the wearer freer in his movements.

In painting, nose-spectacles have given rise to numerous anachronisms. Artists at the end of the Middle Ages and in the Renaissance could not resist representing the Fathers of the Church, in particular Saint Jerome, sporting an invention that came into existence long after their lifetimes.

Many artists thought it only natural to depict scenes from the Bible or antiquity featuring nose-spectacles, a symbol of erudition and culture. Such anachronisms have led some to believe that eyeglasses were invented in biblical times. This pair dates from the eighteenth century.

– 48 –

In the absence of
the eyeglasses, which
would have been
similar to those on
page 26, you will
have to make do with
the case. Cases were
made of a variety
of materials.
The case here is
finely sculpted bone;
note the small ring that holds
the cover closed. On facing page
is a boxwood case; on page 47,
the case is made of copper.

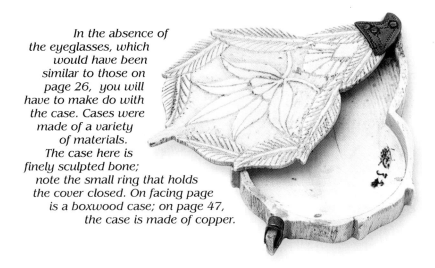

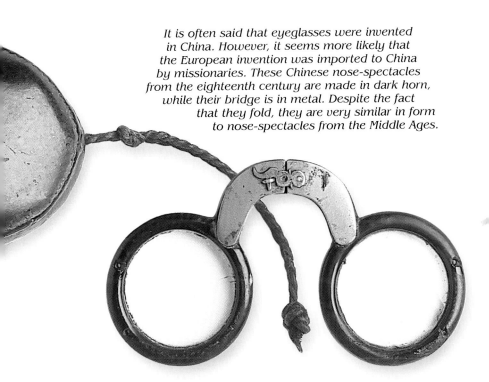

It is often said that eyeglasses were invented in China. However, it seems more likely that the European invention was imported to China by missionaries. These Chinese nose-spectacles from the eighteenth century are made in dark horn, while their bridge is in metal. Despite the fact that they fold, they are very similar in form to nose-spectacles from the Middle Ages.

They might not have actually invented nose-spectacles, but the Chinese were among the first to add ribbons or cords to attach spectacles around the head or ears. Note the sophistication of this shagreen case, decorated with amber beads. The case was carried, as was the custom in China, attached to the belt.

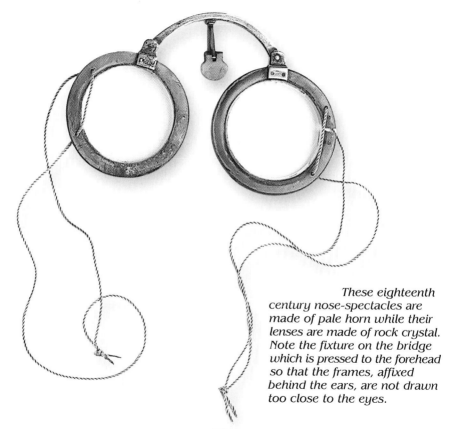

These eighteenth century nose-spectacles are made of pale horn while their lenses are made of rock crystal. Note the fixture on the bridge which is pressed to the forehead so that the frames, affixed behind the ears, are not drawn too close to the eyes.

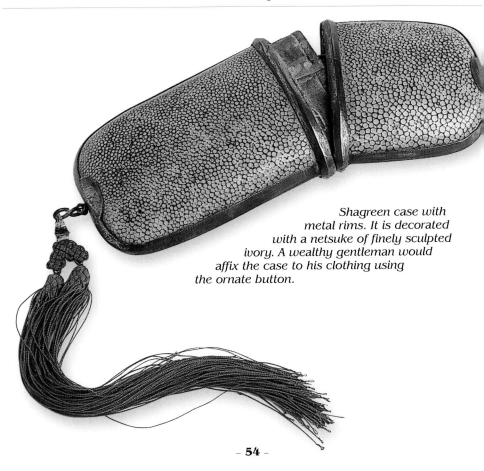

Shagreen case with
metal rims. It is decorated
with a netsuke of finely sculpted
ivory. A wealthy gentleman would
affix the case to his clothing using
the ornate button.

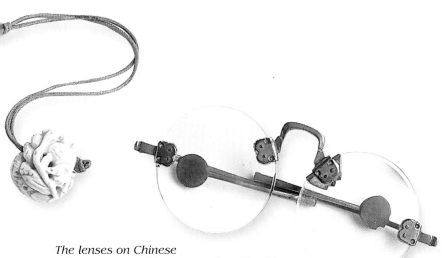

The lenses on Chinese
glasses were seldom corrective, like this
flat rock crystal pair. Rather, they were
worn by dignitaries to add an air of prestige
and importance. The Chinese also believed that
spectacles protected against evil spirits. On this model, it is
worth noting that holes have been made in the glass to attach
the side arms and bridge—a tricky technique at the best of
times, especially given the tools of the era.

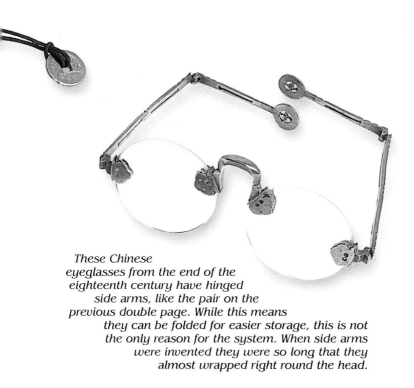

These Chinese
eyeglasses from the end of the
eighteenth century have hinged
side arms, like the pair on the
previous double page. While this means
they can be folded for easier storage, this is not
the only reason for the system. When side arms
were invented they were so long that they
almost wrapped right round the head.

*It was only in the middle of the eighteenth century
that eyeglasses were fitted with side arms.
To begin with they were short and had looped tips
that held the frames in place by pressing the temples.
One of the loops can be seen here protruding
from this pink shagreen case.*

*Sometimes side-arm tips of "temple"
glasses were padded with velvet
to alleviate pressure. This English pair
is made of tortoiseshell. The pair on
the left is horn-rimmed. Both date from
the end of the eighteenth century.*

Before the
system of dual side arms
hinged to the frame was perfected,
some eyeglasses had just one single
arm in the middle (see pages 296 and
297). This late eighteenth century silver
pair has two long, folding side arms
to make them fit their shagreen case nicely.

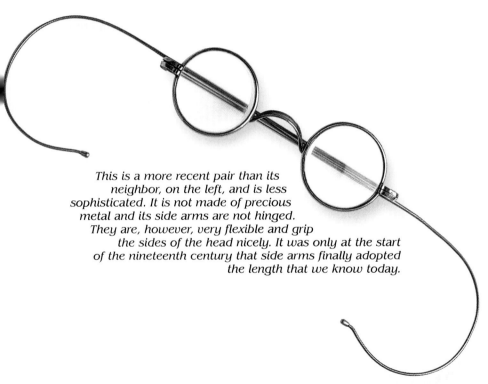

This is a more recent pair than its neighbor, on the left, and is less sophisticated. It is not made of precious metal and its side arms are not hinged. They are, however, very flexible and grip the sides of the head nicely. It was only at the start of the nineteenth century that side arms finally adopted the length that we know today.

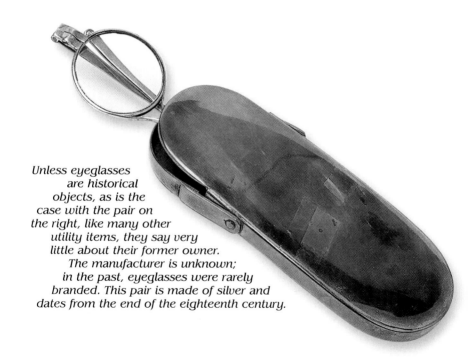

Unless eyeglasses are historical objects, as is the case with the pair on the right, like many other utility items, they say very little about their former owner. The manufacturer is unknown; in the past, eyeglasses were rarely branded. This pair is made of silver and dates from the end of the eighteenth century.

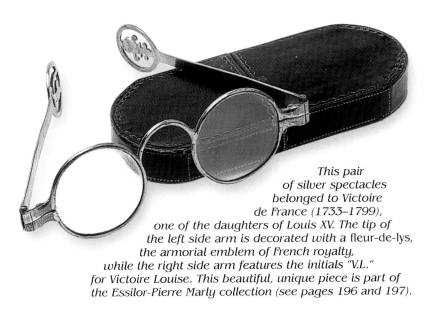

*This pair
of silver spectacles
belonged to Victoire
de France (1733–1799),
one of the daughters of Louis XV. The tip of
the left side arm is decorated with a fleur-de-lys,
the armorial emblem of French royalty,
while the right side arm features the initials "V.L."
for Victoire Louise. This beautiful, unique piece is part of
the Essilor-Pierre Marly collection (see pages 196 and 197).*

As soon as it was accepted that two side arms were
indeed the only proper way to wear eyeglasses,
manufacturers competed with each other to make
them as imaginative and sophisticated as possible.
The side arms on this pair are sliding and so adapt
to different sizes of head. Each has a ring on the tip
to enable them to be worn around the neck.
These eyeglasses are made of silver and date from
the start of the nineteenth century.

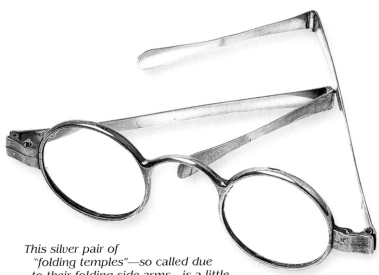

This silver pair of
"folding temples"—so called due
to their folding side arms—is a little
older than that on the facing page (end of
the eighteenth century). During the nineteenth
century, a great many patents were licensed
for a whole range of glasses. Inventors
all believed they had discovered
the ultimate pair.

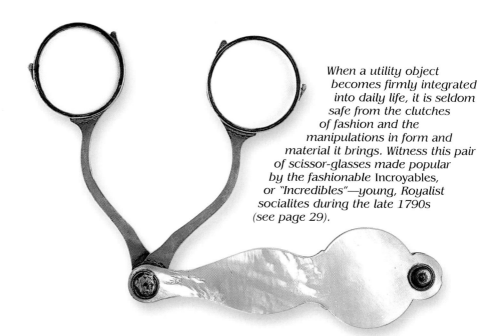

When a utility object becomes firmly integrated into daily life, it is seldom safe from the clutches of fashion and the manipulations in form and material it brings. Witness this pair of scissor-glasses made popular by the fashionable Incroyables, or "Incredibles"—young, Royalist socialites during the late 1790s (see page 29).

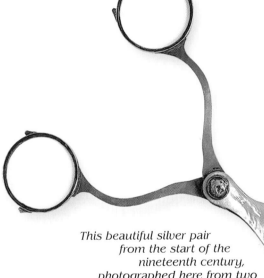

*This beautiful silver pair
from the start of the
nineteenth century,
photographed here from two
different perspectives, folds up
into its mother-of-pearl sleeve which
doubles as a handle. The deployment
of scissor-glasses inspired many
a caricaturist of the era.*

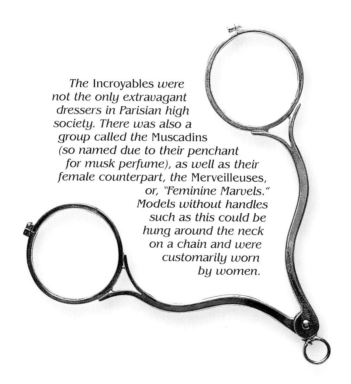

The Incroyables *were not the only extravagant dressers in Parisian high society. There was also a group called the* Muscadins *(so named due to their penchant for musk perfume), as well as their female counterpart, the* Merveilleuses, *or, "Feminine Marvels." Models without handles such as this could be hung around the neck on a chain and were customarily worn by women.*

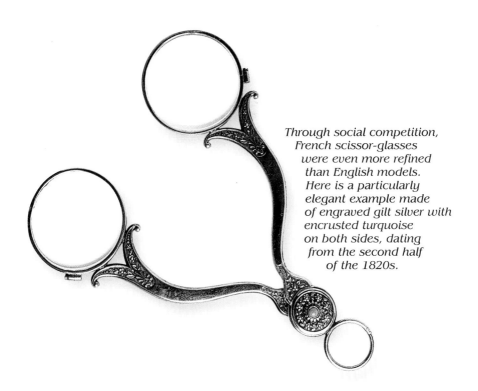

Through social competition, French scissor-glasses were even more refined than English models. Here is a particularly elegant example made of engraved gilt silver with encrusted turquoise on both sides, dating from the second half of the 1820s.

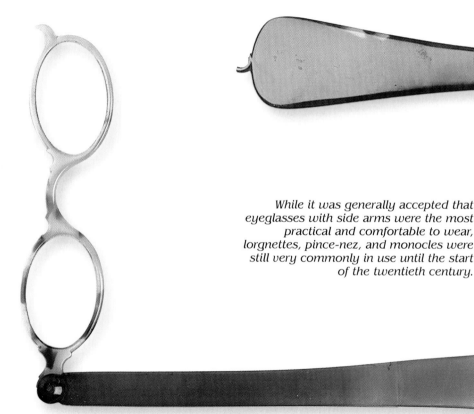
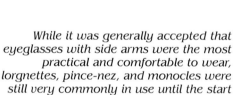

While it was generally accepted that eyeglasses with side arms were the most practical and comfortable to wear, lorgnettes, pince-nez, and monocles were still very commonly in use until the start of the twentieth century.

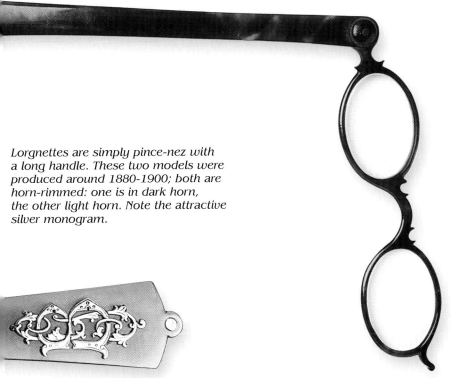

Lorgnettes are simply pince-nez with a long handle. These two models were produced around 1880-1900; both are horn-rimmed: one is in dark horn, the other light horn. Note the attractive silver monogram.

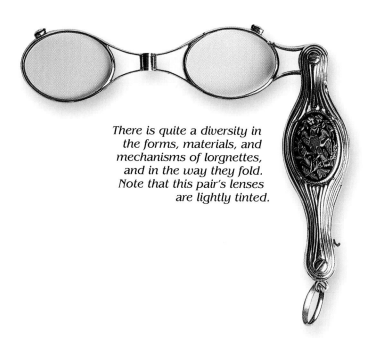

There is quite a diversity in the forms, materials, and mechanisms of lorgnettes, and in the way they fold. Note that this pair's lenses are lightly tinted.

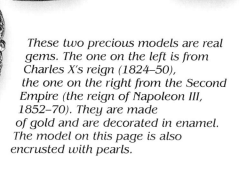

These two precious models are real gems. The one on the left is from Charles X's reign (1824–50), the one on the right from the Second Empire (the reign of Napoleon III, 1852–70). They are made of gold and are decorated in enamel. The model on this page is also encrusted with pearls.

The lenses of many lorgnettes are not in the slightest bit corrective or have only slight magnifying properties. This type of eyeglasses was generally a fashion accessory for posing in public while pretentiously displaying precious metals and stones. Here is a gilt silver model from Napoleon III's time, with an intricate openwork handle.

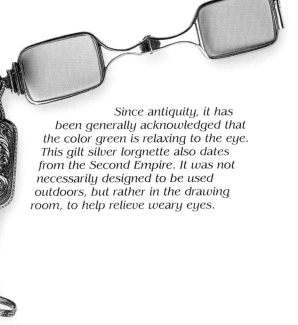

Since antiquity, it has been generally acknowledged that the color green is relaxing to the eye. This gilt silver lorgnette also dates from the Second Empire. It was not necessarily designed to be used outdoors, but rather in the drawing room, to help relieve weary eyes.

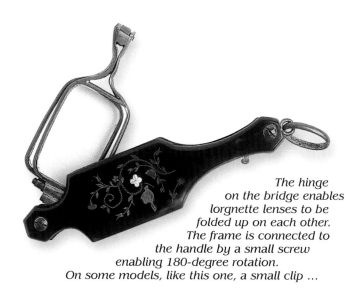

*The hinge
on the bridge enables
lorgnette lenses to be
folded up on each other.
The frame is connected to
the handle by a small screw
enabling 180-degree rotation.
On some models, like this one, a small clip ...*

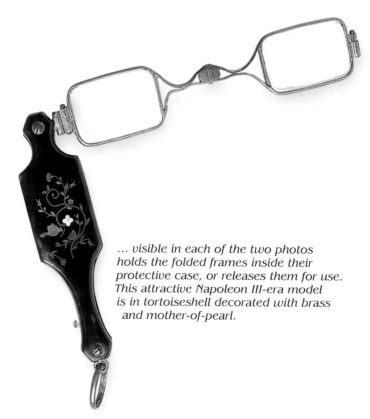

... visible in each of the two photos
holds the folded frames inside their
protective case, or releases them for use.
This attractive Napoleon III-era model
is in tortoiseshell decorated with brass
and mother-of-pearl.

It is said that the fashionable
of the age developed a preference
for the lorgnette over scissor-glasses
(see pages 66 to 69) simply because
the lorgnette, with its handle at the side,
leaves the mouth, in all its beauty, visible;
scissor-glasses, however, with their handle
in the middle, conceal the lips.

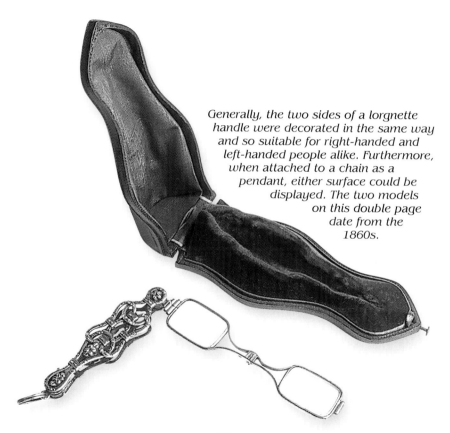

Generally, the two sides of a lorgnette handle were decorated in the same way and so suitable for right-handed and left-handed people alike. Furthermore, when attached to a chain as a pendant, either surface could be displayed. The two models on this double page date from the 1860s.

When it came to style and quality of craftsmanship, Second Empire lorgnettes produced for the upper echelons of society are similar to other utility objects of the era. Sewing, embroidery, and travel accessories, pocket knives and fans were all worked with the same degree of elegance and sophistication.

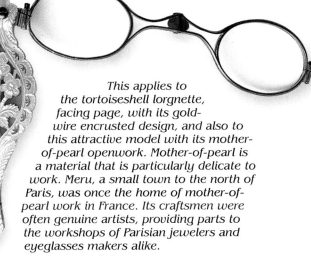

This applies to
the tortoiseshell lorgnette,
facing page, with its gold-
wire encrusted design, and also to
this attractive model with its mother-
of-pearl openwork. Mother-of-pearl is
a material that is particularly delicate to
work. Meru, a small town to the north of
Paris, was once the home of mother-of-
pearl work in France. Its craftsmen were
often genuine artists, providing parts to
the workshops of Parisian jewelers and
eyeglasses makers alike.

Here is another selection from Napoleon III's era, an epoch that produced ornamental objects in large quantities. It is a period that is sufficiently recent for items to still be in good condition. On the left are two engraved silver models. On the right is an enameled gilt silver pair, a light tortoiseshell pair, and, finally, a tortoiseshell model set in silver.

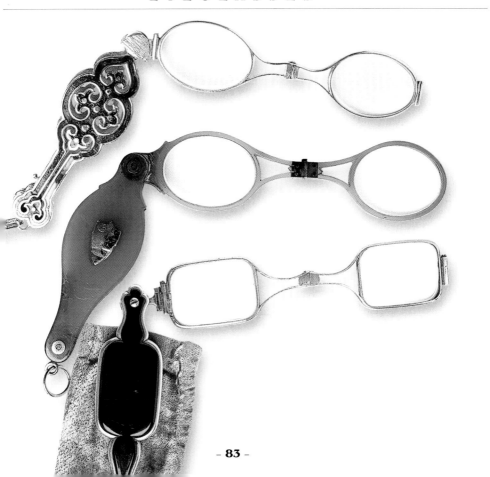

These three lorgnettes date from the 1880s, a later period than those of the preceding double page. On the left is a metal pair. On the top right is a model made of bloodstone encrusted gilt silver, while the example below is made of studded tortoiseshell, with a gold escutcheon engraved with the letters "E.K.B." The shape of the frames and case of the tortoiseshell pair is quite unusual.

From the 1880s to 1900, handles became longer and longer. This lorgnette is made of steel, a material that at the time was considered prestigious. Its ribbon decorations are made of small rose diamonds.

This attractive model, from the 1880s, is made of gold and tortoiseshell. The encrusted initials seem to read "M" and "H." Note on both these lorgnettes the clip in the middle of the handle to hold the folded lenses in their case or to release them for use.

Most metal-rimmed frames were not
made from one continuous loop but were
sealed with a screw. The rims could then
be opened and resealed to replace the
lenses in case of breakage. This screw
still exists on pairs of glasses today,
but it is more discreet and generally
concealed beneath the hinge.

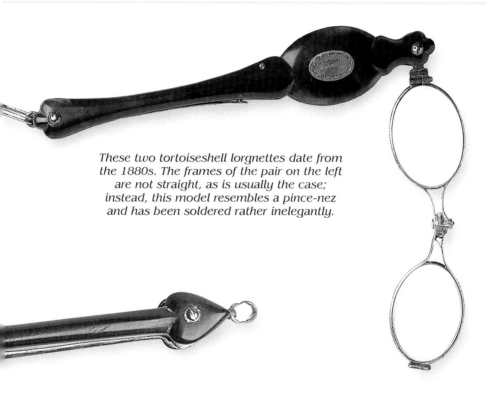

These two tortoiseshell lorgnettes date from the 1880s. The frames of the pair on the left are not straight, as is usually the case; instead, this model resembles a pince-nez and has been soldered rather inelegantly.

The fashion for oval-lensed glasses arrived in France from England in the eighteenth century. Notice that, with older models of nose-spectacles and lorgnettes, the lenses are generally smaller.

There are two main
reasons for this: firstly,
it was easier to avoid
impurities in glass
by cutting lenses of smaller
dimensions, and secondly, the smaller
diameter reduced optical aberrations.
Note the unusual round shape of this folding
lorgnette, as well as its attractive silver
design, topped with a marquis's coronet.

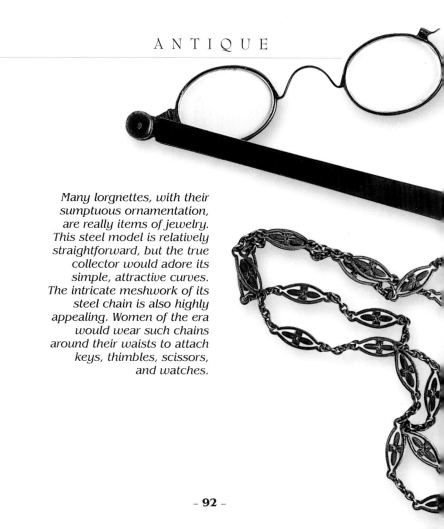

Many lorgnettes, with their
sumptuous ornamentation,
are really items of jewelry.
This steel model is relatively
straightforward, but the true
collector would adore its
simple, attractive curves.
The intricate meshwork of its
steel chain is also highly
appealing. Women of the era
would wear such chains
around their waists to attach
keys, thimbles, scissors,
and watches.

Tortoiseshell lorgnette, the type of which was all the rage in the 1900s. Carrying an object at least a foot long, on a belt or around the neck, cannot have been very practical. The long handle must have been cumbersome for close reading and inconvenient for inspecting knick-knacks. Such are the sacrifices that comfort makes to fashion.

This lorgnette, dating from the 1880s, is made
of attractive pale tortoiseshell, a material that
is not very shock-resistant. When purchasing
a tortoiseshell model, be careful that the rims
or handles have not been patched up.

These two photographs are of the same lorgnette—folded and open in use. The pair is fitted with a cunning system for stacking the two lenses together. The attachment connecting the rims to the bridge is fitted with a spring.

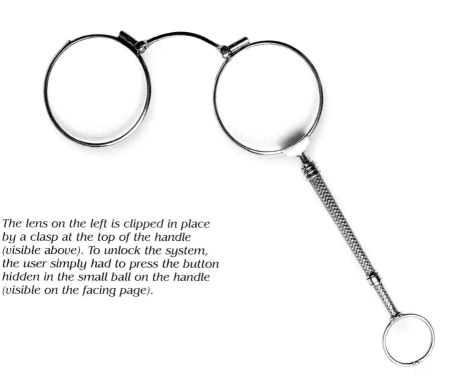

The lens on the left is clipped in place by a clasp at the top of the handle (visible above). To unlock the system, the user simply had to press the button hidden in the small ball on the handle (visible on the facing page).

Like the model on the preceding double page, this lorgnette is made of gold and decorated with enamel. Such pieces are more the result of jewelers' artistry than the craftsmanship of the eyeglass maker. This model was produced by a Swiss jeweler. The two lorgnettes on the facing page are gold-plated. All feature the folding system described on the preceding pages.

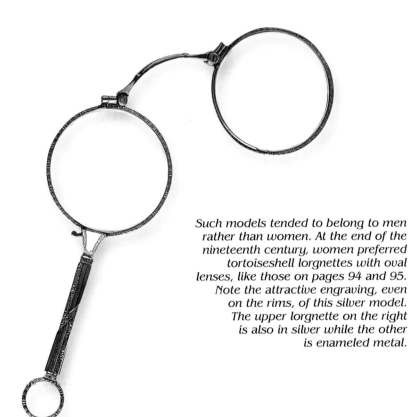

Such models tended to belong to men rather than women. At the end of the nineteenth century, women preferred tortoiseshell lorgnettes with oval lenses, like those on pages 94 and 95. Note the attractive engraving, even on the rims, of this silver model. The upper lorgnette on the right is also in silver while the other is enameled metal.

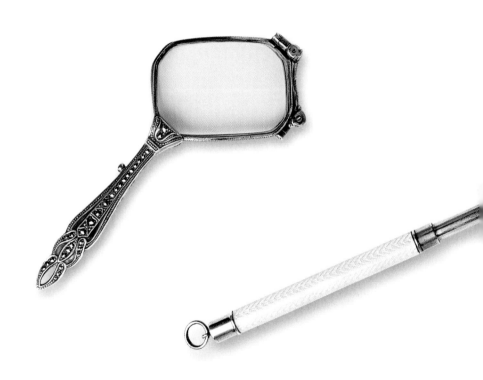

Two silver lorgnettes from the 1880s. The model above has a telescopic handle. Both can be folded away, like the models on the preceding pages. This system, however clever it is, presents one major disadvantage: unlike other examples, such as those shown on pages 88 and 89, the glasses are not protected when the object is not in use.

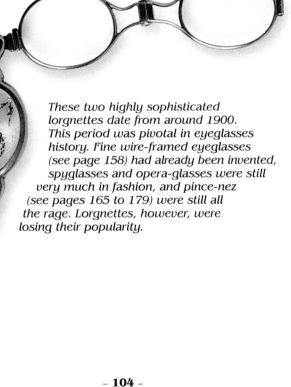

These two highly sophisticated
lorgnettes date from around 1900.
This period was pivotal in eyeglasses
history. Fine wire-framed eyeglasses
(see page 158) had already been invented,
spyglasses and opera-glasses were still
very much in fashion, and pince-nez
(see pages 165 to 179) were still all
the rage. Lorgnettes, however, were
losing their popularity.

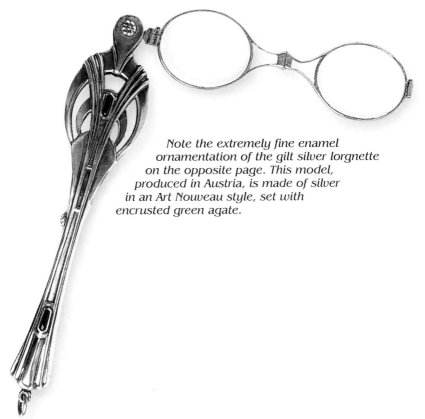

Note the extremely fine enamel ornamentation of the gilt silver lorgnette on the opposite page. This model, produced in Austria, is made of silver in an Art Nouveau style, set with encrusted green agate.

*Two lorgnettes with a hinged bridge from the 1880s.
One is made of tortoiseshell (above) while the other is
made of pressed horn (facing page). Its shape is similar
to that of nose-spectacles. From the "rigid lorgnette,"
to the "hinged lorgnette," to the "spring lorgnette" ...*

*... these pairs represent the next development,
the "open lorgnette," which did not fold away
in a case. The lorgnette is believed in fact
to have been invented by an Englishman,
George Adams, in the 1780s.*

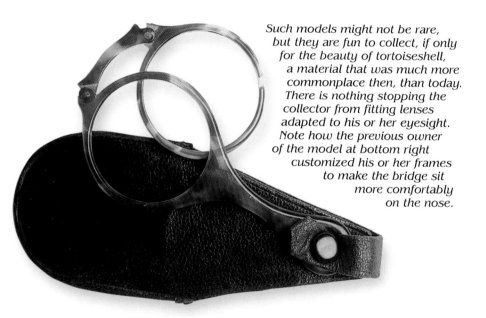

Such models might not be rare, but they are fun to collect, if only for the beauty of tortoiseshell, a material that was much more commonplace then, than today. There is nothing stopping the collector from fitting lenses adapted to his or her eyesight. Note how the previous owner of the model at bottom right customized his or her frames to make the bridge sit more comfortably on the nose.

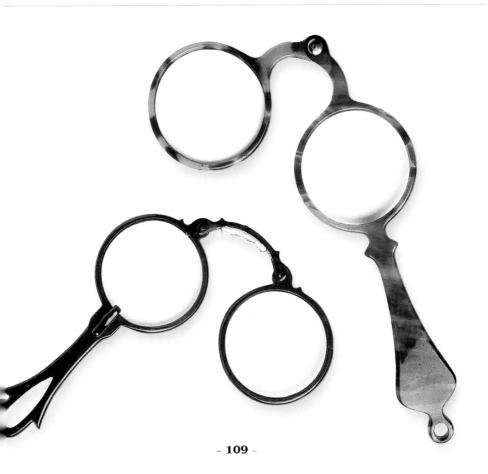

II

MONOCLES AND HANDHELD
eyeglasses

W hile spyglasses, opera-glasses, and magnifying glasses are not really eyeglasses in today's sense of the word, their history is very much bound to that of spectacles. There was a time when all kinds of sight aids were common, and people did not rely on one single type. Even today, nearly all eyeglass collectors possess, among their antique models, several of the optical aids that we will glimpse in this chapter.

This item doubles as
a fan and dance card.
Each prospective partner would write
their name on one of the ivory blades.
It is also fitted with a magnifying glass.
Note the artistry of the miniature.
The reverse side of the handle features the
portrait of a woman. This model comes from
Louis XVI's reign (1774–89) and is part of the
Essilor-Pierre Marly collection (see page 196).

There is no error here!
This is not a page from the
Collectible Corkscrews *volume*
that has been mislaid. The case
of this attractive eighteenth
century pocket corkscrew is
fitted with a small spyglass.

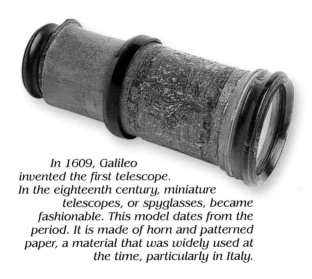

In 1609, Galileo invented the first telescope. In the eighteenth century, miniature telescopes, or spyglasses, became fashionable. This model dates from the period. It is made of horn and patterned paper, a material that was widely used at the time, particularly in Italy.

This attractive fan-spyglass in pale horn dates from the start of the nineteenth century. On objects such as these, the spyglass serves more than just a decorative purpose. The lens may only be small and flat but it is still possible to spy on people without being seen.

*Two canes
equipped with spyglasses.
The spyglass above is made
of copper and ivory, and dates
from the 1830s. The one below
is from the end of the nineteenth
century and includes a compass.*

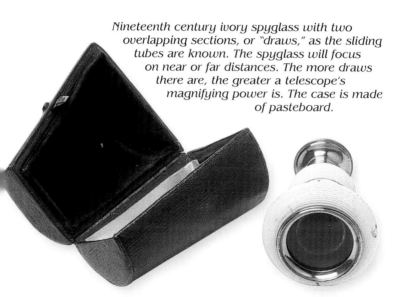

Nineteenth century ivory spyglass with two overlapping sections, or "draws," as the sliding tubes are known. The spyglass will focus on near or far distances. The more draws there are, the greater a telescope's magnifying power is. The case is made of pasteboard.

This rare spyglass of decorated Paris porcelain dates from the nineteenth century. It comes from the same era as many of the eyeglasses and lorgnettes featured in the preceding chapter, as well as many of the magnifying glasses on the following pages.

Due to the fad for eyeglasses in France, the English language borrowed a number of terms from the French. The French called such spyglasses, "lorgnettes," a term that the English adopted for a pair of eyeglasses with a handle. Meanwhile, the French term "pince-nez" (nose-pincher), which passed into English, also coexisted with lorgnon and binocle, the latter not too far from the English "binoculars."

The word "lorgnette" itself comes from the verb lorgner *(to squint).* Lorgner *in turn originates either from the Latin* luscus *(one-eyed) or from the Germanic* luren, *which led to the modern German verb* lauern *(to lurk) and Danish* lure *(to wait in ambush). Today,* lorgner *has come to mean "to ogle." Whether the lorgnette is English or French, like this ivory multi-draw Empire model, ogling was no doubt one of its primary functions.*

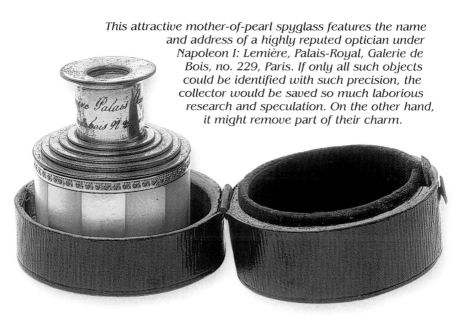

This attractive mother-of-pearl spyglass features the name and address of a highly reputed optician under Napoleon I: Lemière, Palais-Royal, Galerie de Bois, no. 229, Paris. If only all such objects could be identified with such precision, the collector would be saved so much laborious research and speculation. On the other hand, it might remove part of their charm.

Here are two other pairs of spyglasses with dual purposes. The one on the left is fitted to a crystal perfume bottle, while the one on the right accompanies a snuffbox made of walnut burl and lined with tortoiseshell.

*It was also possible for candy boxes, watches, and
sewing accessories to be equipped with spyglasses.
During the Restoration period (1815–30) spyglass
trinkets that could be attached to watch chains,
for example, were very popular.*

Pierre Marly's work on eyeglasses and spyglasses, Lunettes et lorgnettes, *states: "In 1825, it was decided that man had two eyes. This led to the invention, or rather the reinvention, of opera-glasses. The very first pairs of binocular magnifying glasses are described in Father Chérubin d'Orléans's 1677 study in optics,* La Vision parfaite *(Perfect Vision). The glasses were produced in a limited series and were, at some point, forgotten."*

Marly's book is an appreciation of his own collection and was published before the collection was bought by Essilor. These two pairs of opera-glasses are part of it. On the left is a late nineteenth century model, made of ivory and covered in leather, with an unusual oval eyepiece. Below, these telescopic opera-glasses are also made of ivory and date from the start of the nineteenth century.

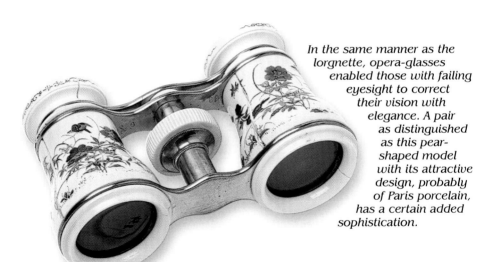

In the same manner as the lorgnette, opera-glasses enabled those with failing eyesight to correct their vision with elegance. A pair as distinguished as this pear-shaped model with its attractive design, probably of Paris porcelain, has a certain added sophistication.

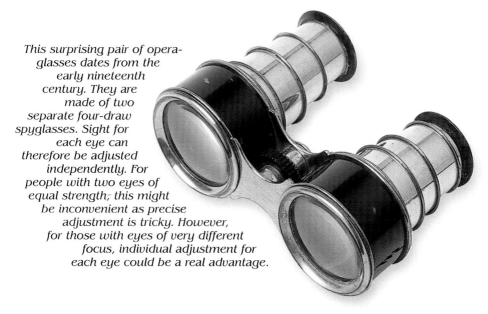

This surprising pair of opera-glasses dates from the early nineteenth century. They are made of two separate four-draw spyglasses. Sight for each eye can therefore be adjusted independently. For people with two eyes of equal strength, this might be inconvenient as precise adjustment is tricky. However, for those with eyes of very different focus, individual adjustment for each eye could be a real advantage.

A rare pair of "skeleton" opera-glasses from the 1830s, reduced to the strictest minimum. At the front, there are two convergent lenses, while behind there are two divergent lenses, hinged for adjustment to the distance between the eyes. Eyesight range is regulated according to the distance of the object under observation, using the wheel underneath the central rod.

Attractive mother-of-pearl opera-glasses in their original case, embossed with the optician's name and address. They are yet further evidence of the immense diversity of the huge family of optical aids. This handful of pages devoted to the subject is a mere introduction to opera-glasses that are so closely related to eyeglasses in both time and nature.

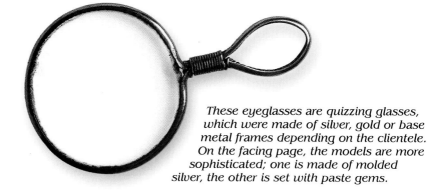

These eyeglasses are quizzing glasses, which were made of silver, gold or base metal frames depending on the clientele. On the facing page, the models are more sophisticated; one is made of molded silver, the other is set with paste gems.

*A quizzing glass is merely
a monocle fitted with a handle,
or a single-lensed lorgnette.
When fitted with a single
convergent lens, to enlarge
close-up objects, they resemble
magnifying glasses. Strictly speaking,
there is a difference between
magnifying and quizzing glasses
in the quality of their finish and
the size of their lenses. Quizzing
glasses have a smaller lens.*

These two delightful models come from the nineteenth century. The one on the left is elegantly decorated with two intertwined dolphins, while the more feminine model on the right is set with semi-precious stones. Both are fitted with rings which suggests they were carried on a chain, attached around the waist or neck.

Like spyglasses and opera-glasses, quizzing glasses come in all kinds of shapes, round, rectangular, or even triangular. They may have handles of differing sizes and ornamentation. This double page is indicative of their diversity. Most date from the nineteenth century. Note the wear and tear of the glass on the model above. Its owner must have been quite a bookworm.

This amusing gilt silver trompe-l'oeil watch is a cross between a pocket magnifying glass and a monocle. The case doubles as a handle when the eyeglass is opened. It would have been an ideal gift for a sophisticated gentleman with waistcoat pockets to fill.

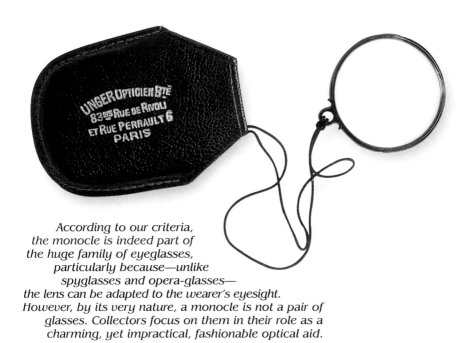

UNGER OPTICIEN B^{TÉ}
83bis RUE DE RIVOLI
ET RUE PERRAULT 6
PARIS

According to our criteria,
the monocle is indeed part of
the huge family of eyeglasses,
particularly because—unlike
spyglasses and opera-glasses—
the lens can be adapted to the wearer's eyesight.
However, by its very nature, a monocle is not a pair of
glasses. Collectors focus on them in their role as a
charming, yet impractical, fashionable optical aid.

*French literature, cinema, and theatrical comedies have
done much for the popularity of the monocle.
The eyepiece was used to portray dignified, austere
or stern characters due to the face an actor has to pull
to hold it in place, an effort that requires a certain
tension in the arch of the brow. The monocle is certainly
an archaic reading aid; what is surprising is that
its height of popularity came as late as
the early twentieth century.*

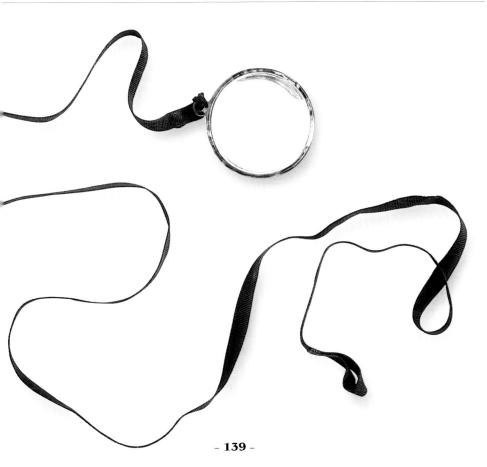

While monocles are uncomfortable to wear, from a purely optical point of view they are not totally absurd. They existed in an age when corrective lenses could not be adapted individually as they are today. So it must have been practical for a farsighted person to be able to see distances and be able to read close-up. Obviously, only one eye could be exercised at once, which is not necessarily ideal.

Monocles were attached to buttonholes by a ribbon or cord. This prevented them from breaking when accidentally dropped. For reasons of comfort, the rims of monocles are always slight in size and, generally, made of gold, silver, metal or tortoiseshell, as in this example.

Amor

LA LUNETTE DE PARIS
C'EST LA LUNETTE D'AUJOURD'HUI

Exigez bien de votre opticien
la véritable lunette "Amor"

Amor *double or 50°/₀*............ 3.800 Frs

Amor *"Cercle"*............ 5.950 Frs

Amor *"Junior"* spécialement étudiée pour
enfants. A partir de............ 1.450 Frs

Amor *or 18 carats, contrôlé par l'Etat*...... 19.500 Frs

Amor *"joaillerie" à partir de*............ 35.000 Frs

Amor *extra légère en or 18 carats*......... 14.500 Frs

LA
LUNETTE
DE PARIS
"Amor"
C'est la lunette
d'aujourd'hui

ÉTIQUETTE DE GARANTIE

En vente chez les OPTICIENS-LUNETIERS SPÉCIALISTES
et naturellement à la Société "LES FRÈRES LISSAC"

III

MODERN
eyeglasses

P rior to the nineteenth century, eyeglasses were reserved for the elite. During the 1800s, corrective lenses became more affordable to the lower classes as hundreds of workshops sprung up producing affordable metal frames. At the start of the twentieth century, new materials appeared. Iron, steel, or nickel could now be combined with celluloid, acetate, or nylon. These new materials enabled an incredible diversification of supply. As eyeglasses became more familiar to the general public, designers began to create them as fashionable accessories. Today this great creativity in eyeglass design and production continues.

Eyeglasses are now so commonplace
that, unless they have eccentric
features, antique yet workaday
pairs of "temples" like these
appear quite normal to us today.
However, up to the mid-nineteenth

century at least, the style-conscious rich
in Europe considered glasses with temples
or sidepieces to be quite inelegant. Good,
practical eyeglasses coexisted with the kinds
of lorgnettes, opera-glasses, and spyglasses
featured in the preceding chapters.

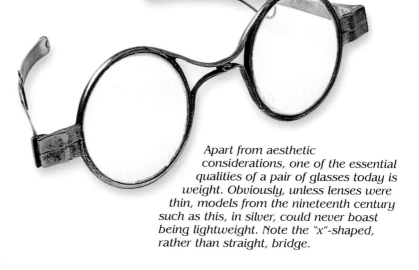

Apart from aesthetic
considerations, one of the essential
qualities of a pair of glasses today is
weight. Obviously, unless lenses were
thin, models from the nineteenth century
such as this, in silver, could never boast
being lightweight. Note the "x"-shaped,
rather than straight, bridge.

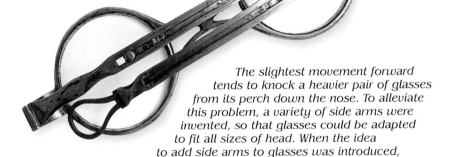

The slightest movement forward
tends to knock a heavier pair of glasses
from its perch down the nose. To alleviate
this problem, a variety of side arms were
invented, so that glasses could be adapted
to fit all sizes of head. When the idea
to add side arms to glasses was introduced,
they were very long, sometimes so much so that
the ends met behind the head.

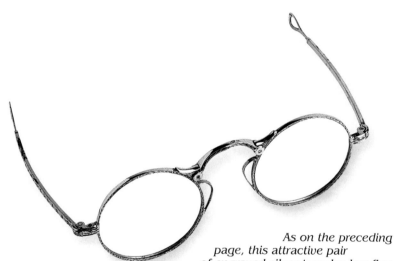

As on the preceding
page, this attractive pair
of engraved silver temples has fine
telescopic side arms. These enable
both adjustment to the contours of the
head and storage in a reasonable-sized case.
Note the nose supports attached to the frame,
a precursor to nose pads.

*Case size was also a prevailing
factor, as with this pair of folding temples.
They were less adaptable for different heads
but could still be put away conveniently in
a case that, if the side arms were not foldable,
would have had to be excessively long.*

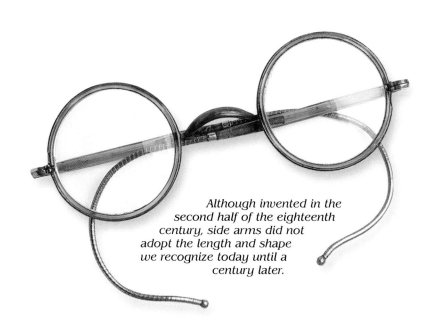

Although invented in the second half of the eighteenth century, side arms did not adopt the length and shape we recognize today until a century later.

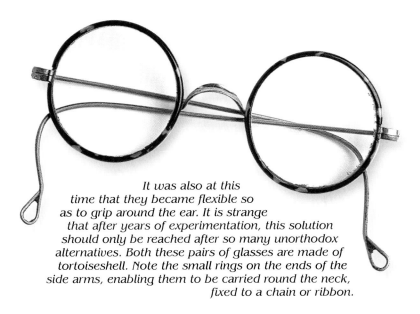

It was also at this
time that they became flexible so
as to grip around the ear. It is strange
that after years of experimentation, this solution
should only be reached after so many unorthodox
alternatives. Both these pairs of glasses are made of
tortoiseshell. Note the small rings on the ends of the
side arms, enabling them to be carried round the neck,
fixed to a chain or ribbon.

An eyeglasses collection always includes a few cases. Some cases are magnificent, like this shagreen example from the eighteenth century. A modest pair of metal spectacles, dating from at least a hundred years later, has taken up residence in it.

*Other cases are made of leather, copper (see page 62),
decorated with pearls (see page 144), embroidered,
in the case of Chinese cases (see following page),
or may be charmingly simple, such as this
small boxwood travel souvenir brought
back from the Brittany resort
La Baule in the 1900s.*

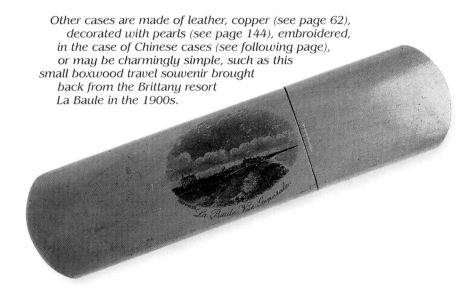

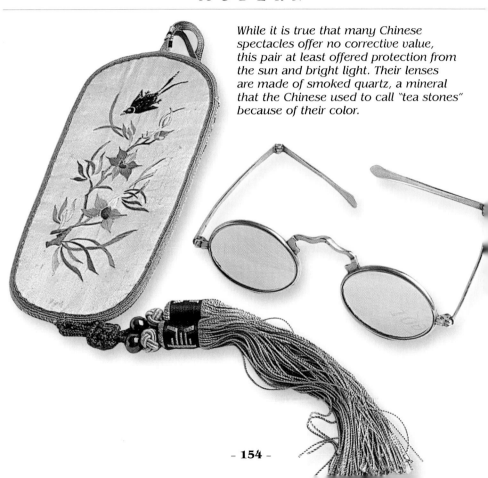

While it is true that many Chinese spectacles offer no corrective value, this pair at least offered protection from the sun and bright light. Their lenses are made of smoked quartz, a mineral that the Chinese used to call "tea stones" because of their color.

Like its neighbor on the left, this pair
dates from the first half of the nineteenth
century. It may look completely European,
but its rock crystal lenses
suggest that it is
in fact Chinese.

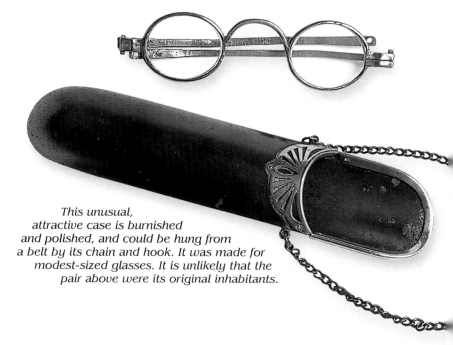

*This unusual,
attractive case is burnished
and polished, and could be hung from
a belt by its chain and hook. It was made for
modest-sized glasses. It is unlikely that the
pair above were its original inhabitants.*

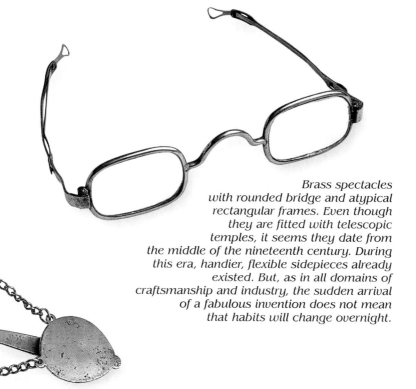

Brass spectacles
with rounded bridge and atypical
rectangular frames. Even though
they are fitted with telescopic
temples, it seems they date from
the middle of the nineteenth century. During
this era, handier, flexible sidepieces already
existed. But, as in all domains of
craftsmanship and industry, the sudden arrival
of a fabulous invention does not mean
that habits will change overnight.

Here is a model that became very fashionable in the nineteenth century: the fine wire-framed eyeglasses we associate with doctors and professors. Due to their lightweight flexibility, these frames, although apparently straightforward, represented a real breakthrough in comfort. The idea that a wearer could forget that he or she had on glasses was now possible.

*These two pairs are equipped with spring hinges,
each made of a small section of rolled metal,
allowing them to open wider. Manufacturers
subsequently greatly improved this system.
Toward 1820, frames of this kind were manufactured
in the village of Les Rousses, near Morez.*

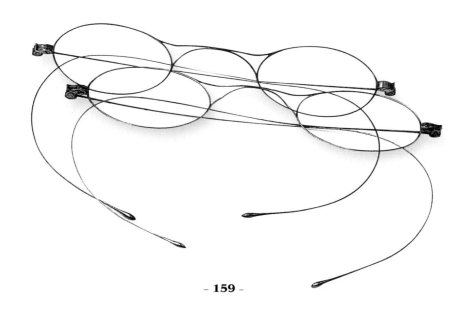

*With simple models
such as these, a true passion
may be born. Such was
the case for collector Jean Melin
(see Acknowledgments), whose
grandmother offered him this humble
pair of eyeglasses that she herself had worn for
years. It only takes two pieces to start a collection.
Jean Melin developed a true passion for his hobby.
In his family and professional life, however, nothing
predisposed him to take up an interest in optics.*

*Jean Melin built up
a magnificent collection over fifty
years. When he learned of plans for this
book, he jumped at the chance to be involved.
Sadly, life dictated otherwise and I am deeply
grateful to his wife Anne-Marie, who shared
her husband's eagerness that his collection
should feature in these pages.*

The kind of simple, no-nonsense frame, made from a variety of metals (brass, iron, even steel and, later, nickel), that Pierre-Hyacinthe Caseaux's workshops were producing in the early nineteenth century (see page 34).

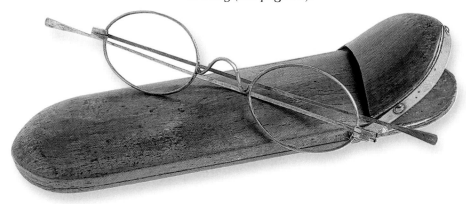

A later pair from around 1850. At the time, small-scale workshops, as in the knife maker's trade, would sell their production wholesale by the gross; that is to say, twelve dozen pairs. Note that, even then, tinted sunshades were available.

An attractive pair
of folding temples
in pale tortoiseshell.
Unlike the kind of models
on the preceding double
page, these more
sophisticated examples
were produced in limited
series, even under
special order.

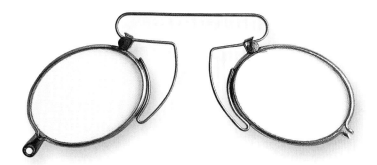

*The pince-nez was fashionable among men
in the second half of the nineteenth century up
to the start of the twentieth. The vogue for the form
is hard to explain as regular frames were already
widely available. In this context, the pince-nez
was a kind of step back in time to discover
all the charm and discomfort of the nose-glasses
of yesteryear (see pages 42 to 51).*

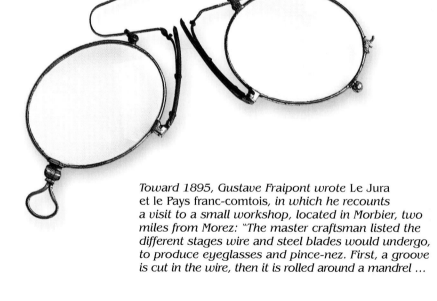

Toward 1895, Gustave Fraipont wrote Le Jura
et le Pays franc-comtois, in which he recounts
a visit to a small workshop, located in Morbier, two
miles from Morez: "The master craftsman listed the
different stages wire and steel blades would undergo,
to produce eyeglasses and pince-nez. First, a groove
is cut in the wire, then it is rolled around a mandrel …

... then it is cut to the desired length to form a ring that is then sealed. Before these rings can be fitted with lenses, various pieces are soldered on with a blowtorch. The frames are then polished using rotating barrels. Each separate piece is punched, tapped, filed and made ready to be fitted with other sections, such as springs or side-arms."

Continuing Gustave Fraipont's text: "It is a measure
of the skill these craftsmen employ that they
manage to earn anything at all when their
wares sell at ten francs per gross.
To us who wear workaday, uncomfortable
pince-nez, so necessary given sight so poor...

... does it ever dawn on us for a moment just how meticulous and complicated their manufacture actually is? Now, when I inspect my eyeglasses, I find a whole host of features I never dreamed existed before, all sorts of little rings, screws, and rivets."

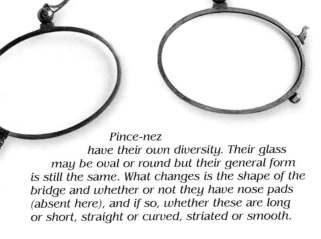

Pince-nez
have their own diversity. Their glass
may be oval or round but their general form
is still the same. What changes is the shape of the
bridge and whether or not they have nose pads
(absent here), and if so, whether these are long
or short, straight or curved, striated or smooth.

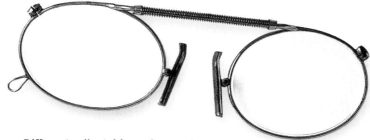

*Different adjustable spring systems can
also change pressure on the nose.
We have grown used to the lightweight,
comfortable glasses of today. In comparison,
wearing a pince-nez for more than five minutes is
an exercise in pain control. Try it for yourself!*

The most common pince-nez are made of iron
or non-precious metals, like those on the previous
pages. Used goods stalls are full of them, costing no
more than a dollar or two. Rarer are examples such as
this finely engraved gilt silver model. The pairs on the
right are made of tortoiseshell. Such frames are hard
to find in good condition. The rims are often split,
or a cord loop or hinge is broken.

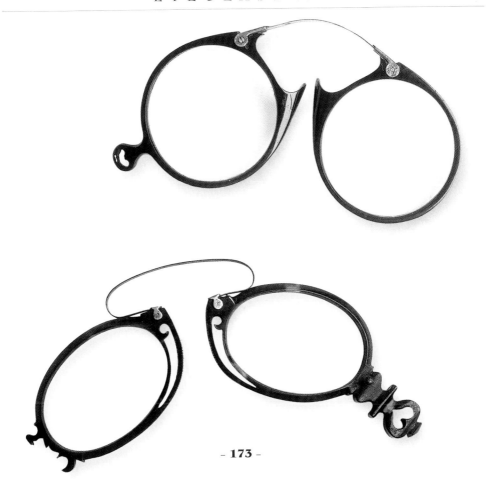

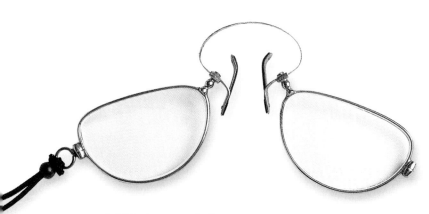

*A fairly long cord slips through the ring on the side
to attach the pince-nez to a buttonhole or watch
chain. In this way pince-nez could fall in safety.
It is worth noting too that, unless different strength
corrective lenses were fitted for each eye
(rarely the case), many pince-nez could be worn
either way round as both sides are generally identical.*

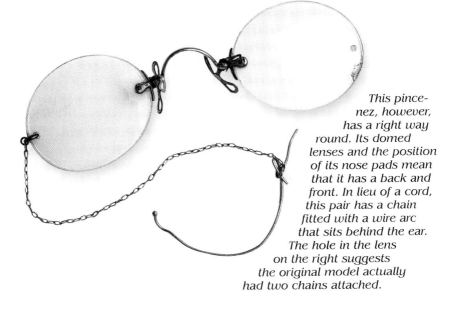

This pince-nez, however, has a right way round. Its domed lenses and the position of its nose pads mean that it has a back and front. In lieu of a cord, this pair has a chain fitted with a wire arc that sits behind the ear. The hole in the lens on the right suggests the original model actually had two chains attached.

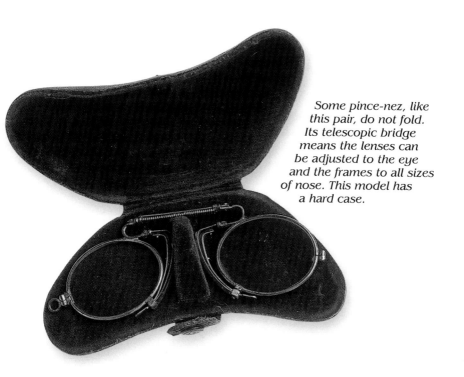

Some pince-nez, like
this pair, do not fold.
Its telescopic bridge
means the lenses can
be adjusted to the eye
and the frames to all sizes
of nose. This model has
a hard case.

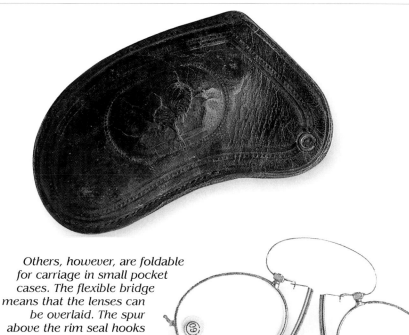

Others, however, are foldable for carriage in small pocket cases. The flexible bridge means that the lenses can be overlaid. The spur above the rim seal hooks onto the cord-ring screw on the opposite rim. In this way both lenses of the pince-nez may be held tightly closed. Note the label, suggesting that this pair have never been used.

In the Middle Ages, during the Feast of Fools in Europe, a carnival that emerged from the pagan traditions of Saturnalia, the hierarchies of society were temporarily turned upside down. People were allowed to mock the ruling classes, nobles, and clerics. The rare pairs of nose-spectacles in existence at the time were worn by men of the cloth, who were deemed to be the vessels of knowledge. Carnival-goers, bearing fool's baubles, would dress up in dunce's caps fitted with bells and sport huge, ridiculous spectacles.

This, and the stigma of novelty, is how spectacles became sometimes associated with madness. That eyeglasses have not always been totally popular in Western cultures is maybe due to these ghosts of the past. This possibly goes some way to explain why lorgnettes and spyglasses, both of which are only fleetingly held in front of the face, were so successful.

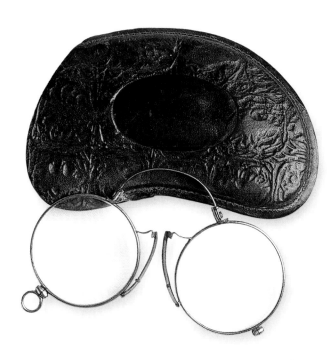

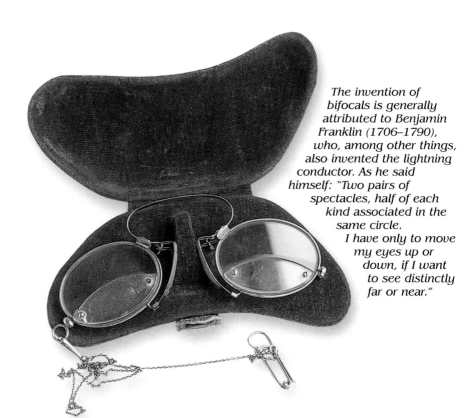

The invention of bifocals is generally attributed to Benjamin Franklin (1706–1790), who, among other things, also invented the lightning conductor. As he said himself: "Two pairs of spectacles, half of each kind associated in the same circle.
I have only to move my eyes up or down, if I want to see distinctly far or near."

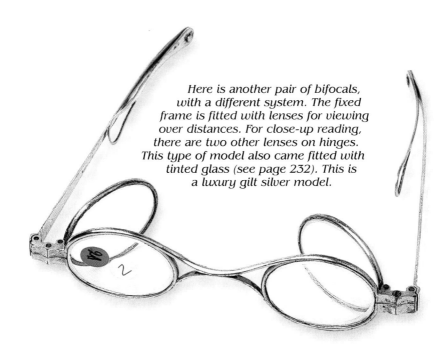

Here is another pair of bifocals, with a different system. The fixed frame is fitted with lenses for viewing over distances. For close-up reading, there are two other lenses on hinges. This type of model also came fitted with tinted glass (see page 232). This is a luxury gilt silver model.

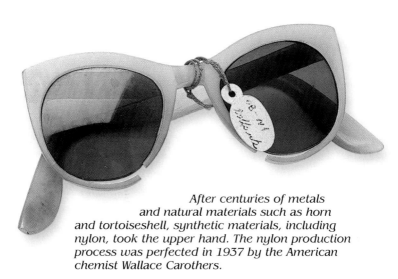

After centuries of metals and natural materials such as horn and tortoiseshell, synthetic materials, including nylon, took the upper hand. The nylon production process was perfected in 1937 by the American chemist Wallace Carothers.

Here are two
  pairs of wire-
    injected nylon
      glasses. The pair
    on the left is probably
    one of the first attempts
      at using the material,
at a time when coloring had
      not been developed. The pair
          above dates from the end of the 1930s,
       tinted in a slightly dreary green-brown color.

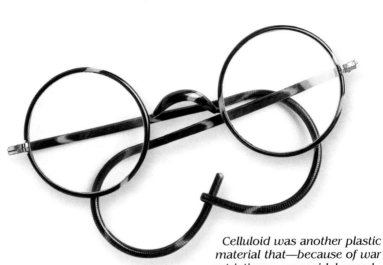

*Celluloid was another plastic
material that—because of war
restrictions—was widely used
during and after the Second World War.
It is produced by plasticizing nitrocellulose with
camphor. It is malleable and easy to color,
but dangerous to use as it is highly inflammable.*

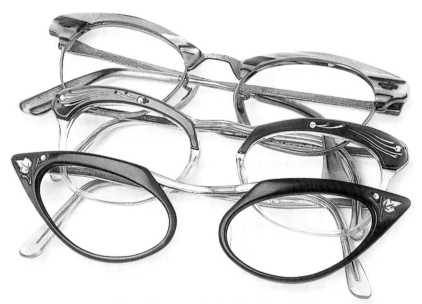

*A series of American-made plastic glasses dating
back to the 1940s. The pair in front is a precursor
of the "winged" eyeglasses that came into fashion
in Europe twenty years later (see pages 196 and 197).*

With this 1947 model, inspired by GI mirror shades,
the designer Georges Lissac brought about a great style
revolution. No newcomer to the profession, he had
already opened a huge optician's store in 1938, in the rue
de Rivoli at the very center of Paris. He was the first
to offer free eye examinations, using the most
advanced technology of the era.

*The lenses of the model are not set in frames,
but are fixed to a frontal bar and supported by small
"shock absorbers" (the French word for which,
amortisseur, spawned the brand Amor). The model
is lightweight and comfortable, as well as strong, and
it was a real innovation from both technical and aesthetic
points of view. Amor frames were initially sold exclusively
in Lissac stores where clients received genuinely personal
service. The style met with huge commercial success.*

*In the face of increasing demand for Amor frames, Georges
Lissac offered the license to manufacture them to his main
supplier, the Société des lunetiers (Essel). This form
of production went against the principles
of the cooperative and the supplier refused.
Georges Lissac was furious and decided to set up
manufacture of the frames himself. In so
doing, he branched out from being a
specialist optician into a fully-fledged
industry, offering his products to other
retailers. A merciless business war broke
out between the two French optics
giants—Essel and LOS (Lentilles
ophtalmiques spéciales), the company
created by Georges Lissac, which later
became LOR (Lentilles ophtalmiques
rationnelles) and finally, after various
mergers, Silor in 1969. Here are six pairs
of Amor glasses in their original cases.*

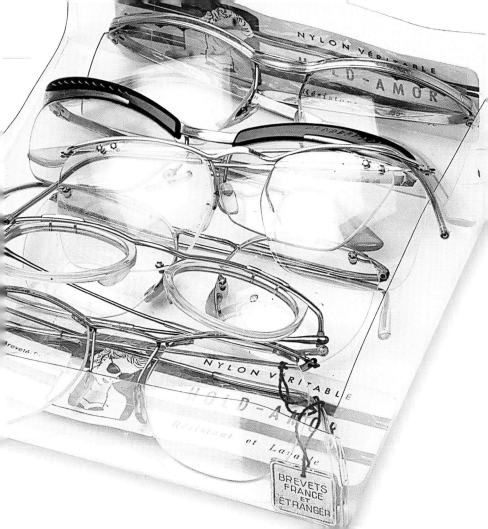

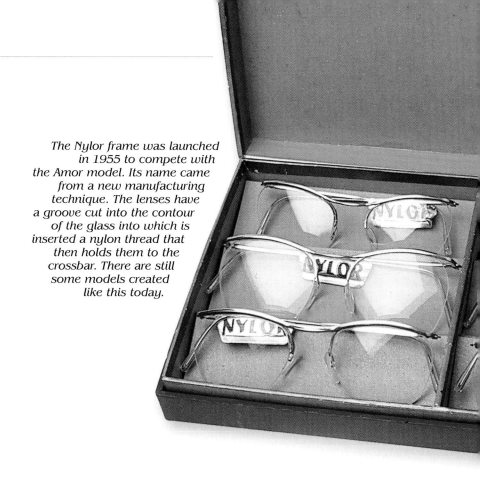

The Nylor frame was launched in 1955 to compete with the Amor model. Its name came from a new manufacturing technique. The lenses have a groove cut into the contour of the glass into which is inserted a nylon thread that then holds them to the crossbar. There are still some models created like this today.

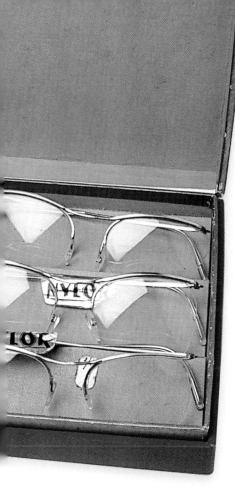

Before the two companies finally merged to produce Essilor (see page 38), the battle between Essel and Silor was not just about frames. They were also in competition in the domain of ophthalmic optics—in other words, lens manufacture. During the 1950s, lens production techniques had advanced in leaps and bounds. In the same year, Lissac released their Orma lenses which were lightweight and unbreakable, while Essel produced the first generation of progressive lenses, the Varilux, developed by Bernard Maitenaz.

*When it was first
launched in 1959,
the Varilux progressive lens was
designed to replace bifocal lenses.
They were called "progressive" lenses
because there is no split between
the near and far view sections. In other words,
their strength varies gradually from bottom to top.*

*From the 1950s and 1960s onwards, the quality
of lenses improved enormously and glasses came
to be made of all sorts of materials.
Here is a pair of sunglasses from
the period; its plastic has not
aged very well.*

*One of the first people in France to realize
that eyeglasses had a future in fashion, now that
most of their technical problems had been overcome,
was Pierre Marly. He was initially employed by the
Lissac Group, where he was in charge of supplies
from 1942 to 1946. He then became head of the
SIL (Société industrielle de lunetterie), a unit located
in Arpajon, south of Paris, which specialized
in the manufacture of plastic frames.*

He obtained his optician's diploma in 1948, and rapidly became, in his own words, an "eyeglasses designer." Royalty, movie stars, and other public figures would look to him for original shades, or have customized models made. Here are two creations from the 1950s. On the facing page is the Plume au Vent model which continued selling for decades afterwards in numerous variations, including gold versions encrusted with rubies or diamonds.

Early in his career, possibly inspired by his creations, Pierre Marly started a collection of antique eyeglasses, optical instruments, engravings, and glasses-related documents.

His collection included more than three thousand
pieces, a part of which used to be on permanent
exhibition in his avenue Mozart store in Paris.
It has recently been purchased by Essilor who
wanted to keep such a valuable
historical heritage in France.
These two "winged" models
from the 1960s were part
of the collection.

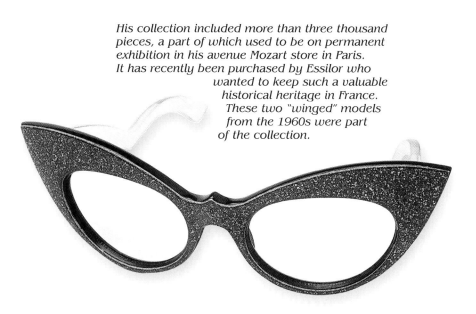

*The Essilor-Pierre Marly
collection has been lent
to the new eyeglasses museum in Morez, where
a number of important pieces will be permanently
on display. Many illustrations in this book feature items
in the collection; there is a list on page 370.*

*These two pairs
are typical of designs from the 1960s, the decade
that heralded the triumph of plastic. Both were
created by Pierre Marly. On the facing page is the
Sofia and on this page is a wrap-around,
highwayman-style "panoramic" model.*

While the 1960s injected a new wild-yet-casual side into female fashions, it also marked a turning point in male fashion. Men began to wear more daring, bolder colors and accessories. This pair of glasses would not go unnoticed.

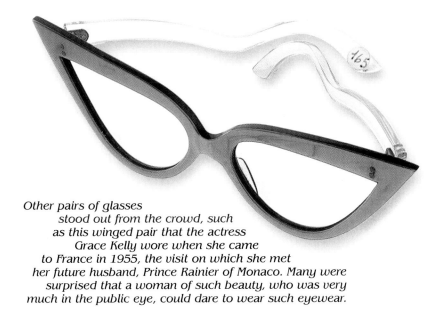

*Other pairs of glasses
stood out from the crowd, such
as this winged pair that the actress
Grace Kelly wore when she came
to France in 1955, the visit on which she met
her future husband, Prince Rainier of Monaco. Many were
surprised that a woman of such beauty, who was very
much in the public eye, could dare to wear such eyewear.*

*In 1947, the current French social security
system was created, bringing together older
forms of health insurance and allowances. Suddenly,
a doctor's prescription was required if a pair of glasses
was to be reimbursed by the state and, by this measure,
opticians could no longer prescribe lenses.*

*Diamond shapes or huge squares are also a possibility,
depending on your taste, shape of face or exhibitionist
tendencies. It is, of course, possible that people
subconsciously choose such large frames to hide behind.
In any case, from the end of the 1960s—when these three
models were produced—onward, it was no holds barred
when it came to form.*

*Celluloid and cellulose acetate were initially used in
eyeglasses manufacture to replace tortoiseshell, which
had become scarce and expensive. The celluloid capital
of France was to be found hundreds of miles from Morez
in the small town of Oyonnax, in southeastern France.
In the eighteenth century, the town had specialized
in the production of horn and tortoiseshell combs.*

*Gradually, manufacturers adopted celluloid and continued
using it until the 1920s. The vogue for shorter hair decreased
demand for combs and the town diversified into children's toys
and glasses parts for Morez's workshops; Morez had always
specialized in metalwork. However, during the Second World War,
Morez was in occupied France, and Oyonnax lay outside this zone.*

Oyonnax's local economy whirred on without hindrance, and many small Oyonnax workshops became full-fledged eyeglasses manufacturers. From the end of the 1950s until the 1980s, Oyonnax was the largest center in Europe for acetate eyeglasses manufacture and even became the main supplier for the American market. Since then recession and international competition have taken their toll.

Nevertheless, Oyonnax remains a center for the production of plastics, working in close partnership with eyeglasses manufacturers, as well as with industries relating to cosmetics and pharmaceutical packing, automobiles, aeronautics, and household electrical appliances. On this and the following double page are wire-injected glasses dating from the period when Oyonnax was the leader in its field.

*As knowledge of plastics became more extensive,
its possibilities grew and grew. The 1960s and 1970s
saw a massive increase in the sale of sunglasses as the
leisure industry in general was expanding. Here is
Pierre Marly's Natacha model which came in several colors.*

In the same era,
fashion designers started
to become aware that everything
from perfume to pens or watches,
and especially eyeglasses, could be turned
into accessories to boost a company's revenues
and image. These glasses were produced
by Emmanuelle Kahn, a key fashion designer
of the 1970s.

This pair, produced by Nina Ricci, was launched
in 1988. Like the perfumes that the fashion house
produces, this model emanates gentleness
and femininity. The lenses are serigraphed with
two doves, the logo of its perfume, L'Air du Temps,
one of the best selling in the world.

*The famous Lacoste crocodile has been wearing
eyeglasses since 1982. The section was created
by Jean-Claude Fauvet, who, before becoming CEO
of the sports and leisurewear company, managed
a small family affair, Cahours de Virgile,
which during the 1970s produced glasses
by the designer Pierre Balmain.*

The Italian group Luxottica was founded in 1961 to produce plastic parts for different sectors of industry, including eyeglasses. At the start of the 1970s, the brand started making glasses itself. Its greatest success came in the 1980s when it produced glasses for Genny, Yves Saint Laurent, Sergio Tacchini, and Armani.

Inspired by
Venetian carnival masks,
these sunglasses were designed by Andrée Putman.
This recent model is already a collector's item, as it is also
signed by L'Amy, who has ceased working with the designer.
Since 2003, he has been replaced by François Pinton.

Above is a model by Chevignon and on the right, one produced by Façonnable, two big names in designer sportswear. If you are interested in collecting important brand names, you have your work cut out for you. As well as those established designer labels, from haute couture to sportswear, there is also a host of other brands not initially connected with fashion.

For example, the automobile makers Jeep (see page 218), Ferrari (see page 278), and Porsche (see page 279) have all produced glasses, as has the Kipling brand of luggage. There are even sunglasses made by candy manufacturer Haribo, as well as those of the doll Barbie and the singer Céline Dion.

This pair, with their unusual
side arms which are
curvaceous when unfolded,
are standard eyewear. They
could well have been included in
the Sports chapter of this book.
They are called Alpine Lite and are
produced by Columbia, a leading
American sportswear manufacturer
and skiwear distributor. It is a brand that
could well make important inroads in France.

*This pair could
have been included
in the Amazing
Eyeglasses chapter.
This is a Pen Reader,
a tiny pair of glasses for
the farsighted, hidden in a pen,
which obviously works perfectly.
The American brand, Microvision,
which produced this model, also made
a version for women—a pair of glasses
hidden in a small aluminum tube resembling
a lipstick or tube of mascara.*

Behind many brand names, however prestigious they might be, lie the real eyeglasses manufacturers who are less well known. These Jeep glasses were produced by L'Amy, which has its own brand of glasses (see pages 224 and 225) and which also has license agreements with Lacoste, Chevignon, Nina Ricci, and Chaumet, among others—fifteen big names in total. Between its interests abroad and its buy-out of Grasset, a key French manufacturer, L'Amy has become the number one eyeglasses producer in France and number ten in the world.

Alain Mikli, another key French designer (see pages 356 to 358),
works with Comotec to produce some of their models. The group
was formed by Christian Receveur, its current CEO, and is the result
of the association of various Morez companies—Finasse, Chevassus,
Sipal, Salino, and Girod, among others—each of whom produces
specific parts for eyeglasses. While these names are not in the public
eye, they have all had a part to play in the history
of eyeglasses manufacturing in the Jura.

*It is not my intention here to list the brand names
to have succumbed to the appeal of designer glasses.
A book would not suffice. The latest fashion house to join
in was Chanel who, in 1999, signed a license
agreement with the Italian giant Luxottica.*

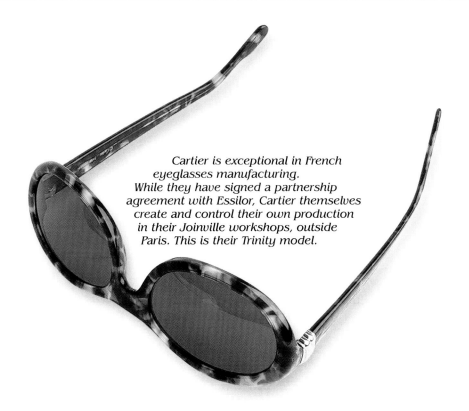

Cartier is exceptional in French
eyeglasses manufacturing.
While they have signed a partnership
agreement with Essilor, Cartier themselves
create and control their own production
in their Joinville workshops, outside
Paris. This is their Trinity model.

For several decades now, special children's ranges
have been developed, with their own colors and forms,
using tough materials, and "flex" hinges to resist (almost)
anything a child might do to them.
Here are two pairs of eyeglasses
produced by Puzzle.

This is another children's pair, this time sunglasses
—a market that has been growing for several years.
Like the adult market, there are many gimmick glasses
which do not offer sufficient protection. There are also
designer names who have developed
their own children's collections.
These pairs are made by
Cébé and Julbo.

*In Morez, Lamy is a fairly
common family name and there are
several eyeglasses manufacturers of this name.
That is why, in 1963, the Auguste Lamy Fils company
decided to set itself apart from the rest by calling
itself L'Amy. The company itself has a long history
and dates back to at least 1810. It would have folded
after the Second World War if Robert and Jacques Lamy
had not admirably breathed new life into it.*

*Marc Lamy, the current CEO of the L'Amy Group,
created the Louis F. Lamy brand as a homage
to the first member of the family to make eyeglasses.
The brand produces high-quality classic eyeglasses
in attractive materials, allying their renowned
savoir-faire with modern technology.*

*While the name
Meyrowitz is usually associated
with the manufacture of pilots'
goggles (see pages 258 to 261),
the brand has also always
had a range of marvelous classic
frames, made to measure from
materials that are rare today.*

On the left
is the model R1 in pale
horn and, this page,
the famous acetate Panto which
also came in tortoiseshell. Natural
materials require a certain maintenance
but they are a real joy to wear and they
often become collectors' items.

IV

SPORTS

eyeglasses

E yeglasses for use in sports are today
becoming increasingly specialized.
The market for sports equipment has expanded
enormously, and now each sport has its own specialized
fashion wear. Manufacturers distinguish leisure
sunglasses from sports models. Eyewear has gone
far beyond the dainty frames and tinted lenses
of the nineteenth century that would protect
the eyes from the sun when one was out strolling,
and far beyond the first goggles for racing or flying.

*This marvelous pair
of snow goggles from
the nineteenth century in
gilt silver and silk belong to the Essilor-Pierre
Marly collection. They are said to have belonged
to the Dalai Lama. It is hard to be certain that they
ever actually shielded any Tibetan spiritual leader's
eyes from the sun, but this hardly matters. The tale
adds to the charm and beauty of the object.*

Today, tinted glasses are associated with the great outdoors, sport, and sunshine, but this has not always been the case. Since antiquity, people have found the color green relaxing for the eyes, believing it to have beneficial properties. Nero and his famous emerald are one example of this (see pages 12 and 13). This pair of tortoiseshell English frames from the nineteenth century might well have simply been worn for "taking it easy."

Ambroise Paré, the great French surgeon of the sixteenth century, also believed that green was good for the eyes. It was for this reason that he made patients recovering from cataract operations wear green clothing or green-tinted lenses. Three centuries later, this pair was possibly fashioned for the same reason. The dual set of lenses functions like bifocals (see page 181).

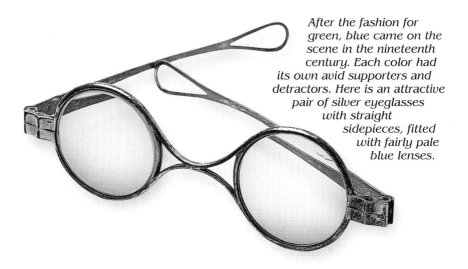

After the fashion for green, blue came on the scene in the nineteenth century. Each color had its own avid supporters and detractors. Here is an attractive pair of silver eyeglasses with straight sidepieces, fitted with fairly pale blue lenses.

In Good Society, *a lifestyle guide published in London in 1860, an anonymous countess is cited as saying: "If it is absolutely necessary to wear eyeglasses, their lenses should be as slight as possible and in yellow or steel blue. If the eyesight is weak, blue or smoked tinted glass is more suitable. Green lenses are utterly loathsome!" These two pairs of eyeglasses from the epoch in question would perhaps have met with the countess's approval.*

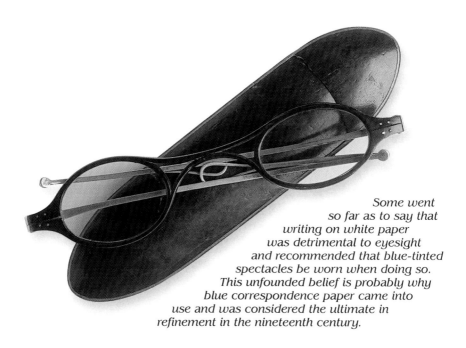

*Some went
so far as to say that
writing on white paper
was detrimental to eyesight
and recommended that blue-tinted
spectacles be worn when doing so.
This unfounded belief is probably why
blue correspondence paper came into
use and was considered the ultimate in
refinement in the nineteenth century.*

*Philosophers and
scholars from the past—including
the great Pascal—often decried eyeglasses
as «deceitful trickery», which deformed reality
and, therefore, truth itself. It is not hard to imagine
what they thought of people who saw life through
blue-tinted spectacles (or pince-nez), let alone
gray- and orange-tinted ones, examples of
which are on pages 240 and 241.*

There are many anecdotes from
the past about the virtues of tinted
glasses, demonstrating the sense of
humor or gullibility of their users.
It is said that the French songwriter
Antoine Désaugiers (1772-1827)
wore red-lensed glasses until the
end of his life, to create the
illusion of looking through
a wineglass, as his doctor
had forbidden him to drink.
Other tales tell of thrifty peasants
who would cover the eyes of their
horses with green-tinted spectacles
at feeding time so that the horse would
eat its straw thinking it was hay.

*There were also intellectuals who believed that night
was for thought and day for action, so would wear
dark blue lenses to blur night and day.
This monocle and pair of glasses might have
suited them very nicely.*

*This particular orange-brown
color was named after its inventor,
Doctor Louis Fieuzal (1836-1888), who was
head of the Quinze-Vingts hospital in Paris, a famous
institution specializing in eye care.*

*Whether fashioned for home wear or to protect the eyes
while out walking, boating, or cycling, the range
of colored lenses offered by nineteenth century
opticians is impressive. There were up to eight different
shades of gray, ten of blue, six of green or brown, and
five of orange. There were even red lenses available.*

An attractive pair of tortoiseshell
glasses from the early 1900s.
With the development of transport and
tourism, eyeglasses that offered effective
sun protection became more widespread,
and were de rigueur when taking a train to
a spa town or the seaside. Note the air vents
where the side shields meet the rim,
so that the glasses do not fog up.

*This pair
could be affixed
to small hooks on a pince-nez or
a pair of corrective lenses. The size of the
bridge is adjustable and there are small metal nose
pads to provide support on each side of the nose.*

Goggles for cyclists, motorcyclists, motorists,
and pilots were a great novelty in the twentieth
century. We can be certain that this kind
of eyewear was actually worn for sport.
Before leather and rubber were used, goggles
were made of fabric, generally silk...

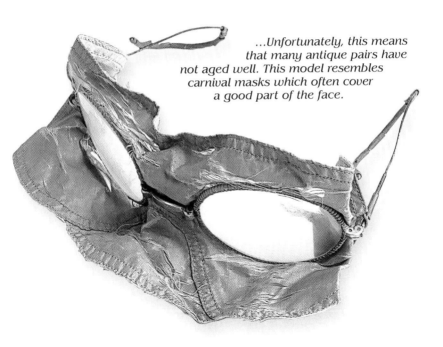

...Unfortunately, this means
that many antique pairs have
not aged well. This model resembles
carnival masks which often cover
a good part of the face.

My great-grandfather, Louis Crestin-Billet, was one of the first Frenchmen to make eyewear for motorists and pilots. He founded his business in 1892 with two of his brothers, producing metal eyeglasses and pince-nez, for which he won a gold medal at the 1893 World's Fair in Chicago.

Several years later,
he received a visit from Baron Benz,
founder of Mercedes-Benz, who asked
him to produce two pairs of eyeglasses,
one for himself and one for his dog when out
motoring! This type of eyewear first featured in the
1906 catalogue. In 1927, my great-grandfather changed
his business's name to Cébé, which is how the initials
of his last name (C.B.) are pronounced in French.

Like many other utility objects produced during the nineteenth and twentieth centuries, eyeglasses are often without indications of brand name or origin. When there is some kind of identifying sign, it is often mysterious. Here, the initials "J.B.J." are accompanied by the French words brevet déposé *(patented). They are clearly not the initials of their owner.*

Appearances can be deceptive. A pair of glasses like these might appear old, which is probably the case here. But the Manufrance catalogue of 1965 still featured a very similar model with rubber side shields instead of silk.

While today manufacturers market glasses for specific sports, in the past models were not necessarily channeled into a niche market. In the 1930s, a well-known brand, Oto, on the opening page of its catalogue, boasted that it made eyeglasses for aviators, motorists, motorcyclists, and cyclists, and that it specialized in eyewear and visors for all sports.

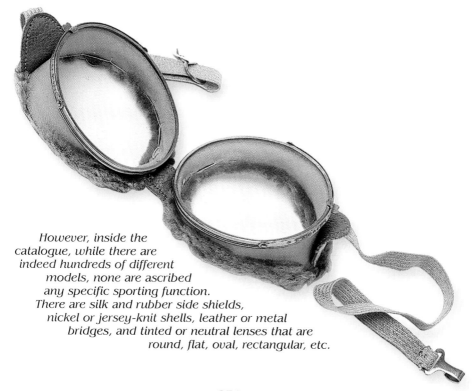

However, inside the catalogue, while there are indeed hundreds of different models, none are ascribed any specific sporting function. There are silk and rubber side shields, nickel or jersey-knit shells, leather or metal bridges, and tinted or neutral lenses that are round, flat, oval, rectangular, etc.

*From the early twentieth century, leisure automobiles
as opposed to racing cars had closed tops and the eyes
no longer needed protection from dust. However,
headlamps from other cars remained a problem. In the
mid-1920s, this pair of Lynx glasses offered some relief.
They were fitted with little foldable blue lenses, and cost
45 francs, the equivalent of 30 dollars today.*

A driver's field of vision was very different depending
on whether he was wearing wide or round lenses.
Note the panoramic vision afforded by the model on the facing
page. Here it is folded in two. Some goggles were fitted
with hinged tinted lenses, which could be flipped over
to offer relief from brighter lighting.

This model came with a leather or a metal-hinged nose bridge so that it could be folded up into a case or pocket easily. They are known as «collapsible» glasses.

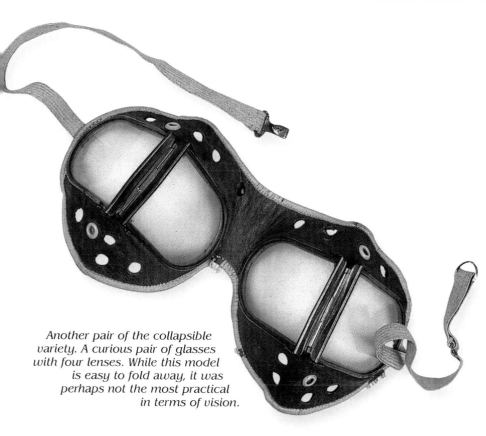

Another pair of the collapsible variety. A curious pair of glasses with four lenses. While this model is easy to fold away, it was perhaps not the most practical in terms of vision.

Although many pairs of glasses remain anonymous, this pair is easy to identify. There were made by Meyrowitz, a name that has been part of the eyeglasses trade since 1875, when Emile Bruno Meyrowitz, a Lithuanian immigrant, started selling glasses in the streets of New York. Five years later, he opened a shop in Albany and produced a mail-order catalogue. He ended up manufacturing his own products.

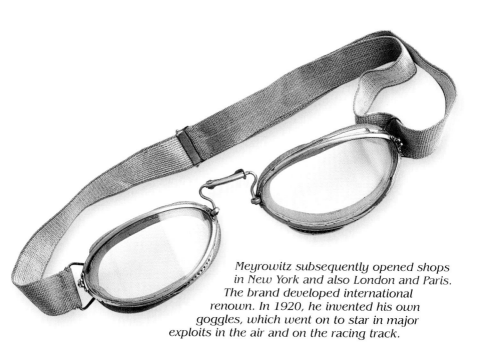

Meyrowitz subsequently opened shops in New York and also London and Paris. The brand developed international renown. In 1920, he invented his own goggles, which went on to star in major exploits in the air and on the racing track.

The greats of aviation—Charles Lindbergh, Charles Nungesser, Jean Mermoz, and Maryse Bastié—as well as the drivers of top teams like Alfa Romeo, all wore Meyrowitz protective eyewear. Note this pair with a flip-up visor.

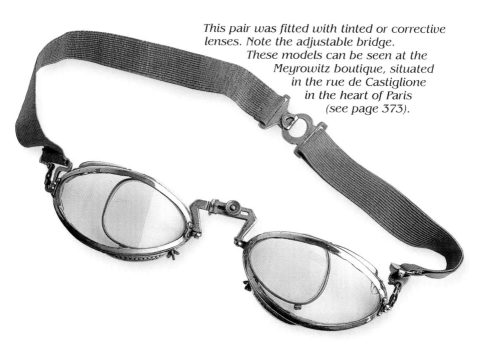

This pair was fitted with tinted or corrective lenses. Note the adjustable bridge. These models can be seen at the Meyrowitz boutique, situated in the rue de Castiglione in the heart of Paris (see page 373).

*Contrary to appearances, these are actually brand
new eyeglasses. They are a re-release of the Aviator
Goggles model created by Léon Jeantet, in Morez,
in 1929. Pierre-Léon Sirven, a grandson
of Léon Jeantet, decided to reissue
this item in 1992.*

The Jeantet company's current range is manufactured in the same location with the same tools as the original models. The colors and graphics on the label are also faithful reproductions of those known by the past pilots who used these goggles.

Two pairs of eyeglasses produced by the Italian brand Protector. The pair below belonged to a French rally driver, Georges Grignard. His career started in 1925 and he competed in a number of rallies. He came fifth in the 1949 Le Mans 24 Hours contest in a Delahaye car.

*It is rare to find drivers' goggles in a good state of repair.
Either because they have been well used in a long,
tough career or because their materials do not age well.
Rubber dries out or elastic becomes slack—as in the
case of this pair here. Sometimes the lenses, when they
are tinted, lose their color. A great many pairs were
made of celluloid or cellulose acetate.*

Even where they have lost their original optical residents, attractive iron cases are always a joy. This case was made in France, even though the writing is in English. The name "goggles" originates from the English verb "to goggle"—"to stare with wide and bulging eyes". The term is also applied to any pair of eyeglasses of outsized proportions.

This case contained drivers' goggles manufactured in Morez. Oto was the brand of the Consortium général d'optique. The CGO logo is written curled up inside the hot air balloons. The case came in other colors—notably red for the Eclipse model, but also blue.

*English goggles produced
by Stadium. This pair was sold
during the 1960s for motorcyclists.
Like many other models of the same type,
they seem to be based directly on goggles
originally designed for the army ...*

... such as
these tank goggles,
apparently from the same
factory. They are made of painted brass and
fitted with wide lenses to allow for panoramic
vision. Their width can be adjusted by the sliding
metal ridge over the leather nose bridge.

American army goggles produced by Stemaco Products Inc., in Port Huron, Michigan. The instructions state that they are effective against sun, wind, and dust. They were supplied with neutral and gray-tinted lenses. While they were in widespread use during WWII, they were not the only model of its kind available.

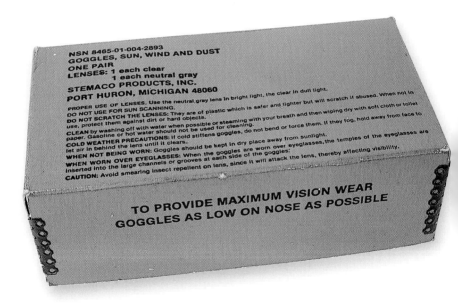

NSN 8465-01-004-2893
GOGGLES, SUN, WIND AND DUST
ONE PAIR
LENSES: 1 each clear
1 each neutral gray
STEMACO PRODUCTS, INC.
PORT HURON, MICHIGAN 48060

PROPER USE OF LENSES. Use the neutral,gray lens in bright light, the clear in dull light.
DO NOT USE FOR SUN SCANNING.
DO NOT SCRATCH THE LENSES: They are of plastic which is safer and lighter but will scratch if abused. When not in use, protect them against dirt or hard objects.
CLEAN by washing off with water when possible or steaming with your breath and then wiping dry with soft cloth or toilet paper. Gasoline or hot water should not be used for cleaning.
COLD WEATHER PRECAUTIONS: If cold stiffens goggles, do not bend or force them. If they fog, hold away from face to let air in behind the lens until it clears.
WHEN NOT BEING WORN: Goggles should be kept in dry place away from sunlight.
WHEN WORN OVER EYEGLASSES: When the goggles are worn over eyeglasses,the temples of the eyeglasses are inserted into the large channels or grooves at each side of the goggles:
CAUTION: Avoid smearing insect repellent on lens, since it will attack the lens, thereby affecting visibility.

TO PROVIDE MAXIMUM VISION WEAR
GOGGLES AS LOW ON NOSE AS POSSIBLE

Racing drivers would wear army surplus goggles in early Formula One competitions. The great Scottish driver, Jim Clark, wore them up to the end of his career. Photos of him taken at the French Grand Prix at Le Mans, in 1967, show him sporting just such a pair. He would often stick a strip of black tape over the upper part of the mask.

From the 1960s onwards, polyurethane replaced silk and rubber side shields that had been used till then. This is a pity for collectors, as this initially innovative material resists the ravages of time less well than its predecessors. In a few years, there will probably be nothing left of this mask and its crumbling shield.

*This mask was used by parachutists until 1970.
It is signed Rod, a brand made by the Morez-based
manufacturers Grandchavin-Lamy. The company
was bought out by Cébé in 1988.*

To begin with, Ray-Bans were made for pilots. In the
1960s and 1970s, young people around the world
dreamt of acquiring a pair—wearing them meant
sharing a part of the American dream and for just
a moment believing oneself to be a Hollywood star.
Their myth has by now lost some of
its appeal, however.

Ray-Ban is a brand name once belonging to the American firm Bausch & Lomb, an optical establishment founded in 1853 by two German immigrants. It was one of the first manufacturers to make rubber eyewear and produce a pair of sunglasses for soldiers in WWI. The company also invented fixed focus polarized lenses. Today Bausch & Lomb only make contact lenses and ophthalmologic products. Ray-Ban was bought out by the Italian giant Luxottica.

*The success
of Ray-Bans has inspired many
manufacturers who copy their
frames more or less wholesale.
Quality is not always up to scratch but
this is not necessarily an issue when you are
wearing that famous "pilot-shaped" frame.*

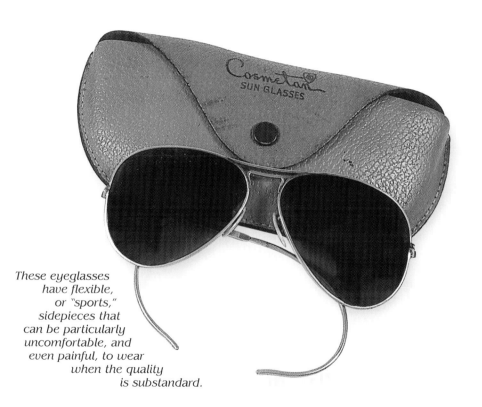

These eyeglasses have flexible, or "sports," sidepieces that can be particularly uncomfortable, and even painful, to wear when the quality is substandard.

This is a real collector's item as these Ferrari shades are no longer produced. If you really want to offer such a pair as a gift to your own cavallino rampante (rearing stallion), you will have to make do with a second-hand pair.

However, if you have a penchant for German cars,
you might like these attractive Porsche glasses.
They are similar to the pilot frames but carefully
redesigned. This model is produced in the workshops
of the eyeglasses manufacturer Rodenstock.

Tag Heuer is the result of the partnership of the Swiss watchmakers, Heuer, and the Swiss technologies specialist, Techniques d'Avant-Garde. This model, released in May 2002, has met with great success, a triumph for the encounter of design and technology. It is manufactured by Logo, a company formed from the merger of the Darnaud group and Essilor's former frames division.

*This model has both
comfort and a classy design.
The sidepieces of these eyeglasses
are attractively covered in leather.
Produced by Histoire de voir, a brand
created in Paris by the designer,
Stéphane Sarnin.*

In 1948, Henri Oreiller won the downhill ski event at the Saint Moritz Winter Olympics in Switzerland while wearing a pair of Cébé goggles. This prompted the brand to develop their ski and mountain range. This very classical pair of glacier glasses has been available for years.

*A model signed by another skiing champion,
Jean Vuarnet, who won the downhill race at the 1960
Squaw Valley Winter Olympics. This range was produced
by the optician Roger Pouilloux who claimed they offered
the best protection in the world. They were
phenomenally successful up until the 1980s.*

Cébé ski mask. This classic design barely changed between the end of the 1960s and the 1990s, when this model was produced. Cébé merged with a Swiss group in 1993 and today also makes watches, helmets, and ski gloves.

*When it comes
to ski masks, the current trend
is for the techno-retro look.
This applies to equipment
for all ski-related sports that have
sprung up over the last fifteen years, such as
snowboarding, surfing, and other extreme activities.
This model is made by Demetz, a brand specializing
in sports eyewear (see pages 290 and 291).*

This may look like an instrument of torture, but it is in fact a pair of glasses for competitive shooting. They enable vision through one eye without having to hold the other eye closed, giving an aiming axis parallel to the optical axis of the lens. The workshops of Jules Guillaume, in Morez, have today disappeared, but such eyewear was their specialty.

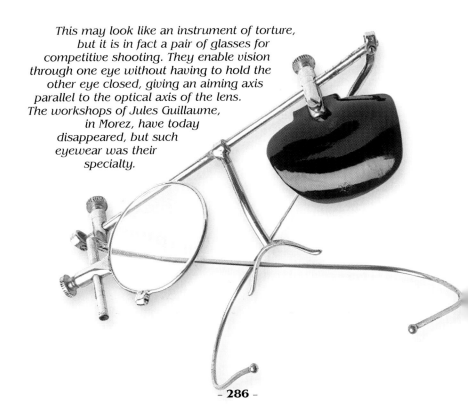

Specially designed for clay pigeon shooting or hunting, these spacious eyeglasses were made by the American brand Randolph. Orange and yellow lenses enhance contrasts. This is a recent model.

Adidas has developed a range of eyeglasses for use by aficionados of mountain biking and golf. This Gazelle model is for the avid golfer. It is lightweight, offering all-round cover. It is also fitted with a handy clip for the optional attachment of corrective lenses.

In 1975, the American Jim Janard invented a revolutionary material, unobtainium, for use in motorcross bike manufacture. From 1980 onwards, he decided to apply his research to the area of eyeglasses and created the brand Oakley, which immediately developed mythical status among the young. The champion cyclist, Greg LeMond, sponsored by Oakley, largely contributed to the success of the brand's Eye Jacket model, which is more recent than this particular pair.

Founded in 1950 by Roger Demetz—an optician and professional diver—the French Demetz company pioneered the development of optical swimming goggles. Gilles Demetz took over from his father in 1988 and regularly wins awards for his innovations.

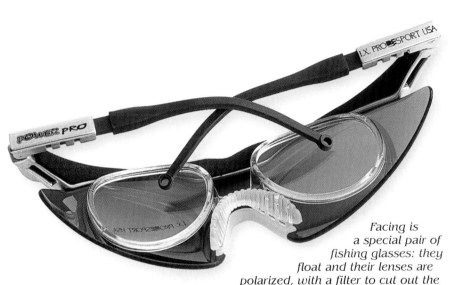

Facing is a special pair of fishing glasses: they float and their lenses are polarized, with a filter to cut out the reflection of the sun on the water. Here is another Demetz model—protective eyewear fitted with corrective lenses. They may be used for fishing or hunting as well as in scientific laboratories.

*This pair of swimming goggles was made in Taiwan
and their quality is not their strong point.
In the domain of sports eyewear, the finest high-tech
luxury designs cohabit with inferior copies.
Collectors of the future will have their work
cut out for them.*

And finally, a touch of humor—windshield-wiper
glasses from the 1970s. At the time the motor
system that operated them was rather cumbersome
and impractical. Much progress has since been
made in miniaturization. This could be
a fun idea to recycle.

V

AMAZING
eyeglasses

P eople have an instinct for taking an existing object
and adding extra functions to "improve" it, whether
in the name of utility or fashion. Eyeglasses have
not escaped this mania. This chapter features antique
spectacles as well as modern curios, genuine eyewear
and professional optical instruments, from throughout
history, in all shapes and sizes—each model has its own
eccentric touch. It offers a glimpse of the expression
of those creators and inventors, and the ingeniousness
and distinction that a passion for their art has produced.

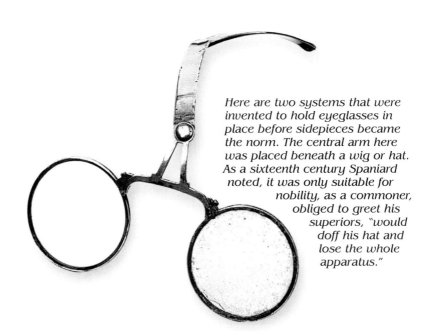

Here are two systems that were invented to hold eyeglasses in place before sidepieces became the norm. The central arm here was placed beneath a wig or hat. As a sixteenth century Spaniard noted, it was only suitable for nobility, as a commoner, obliged to greet his superiors, "would doff his hat and lose the whole apparatus."

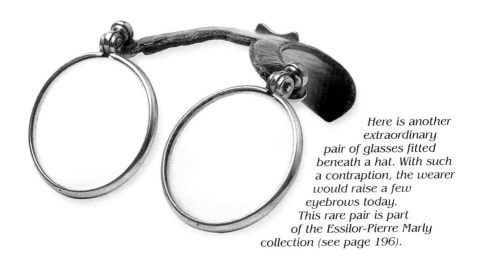

*Here is another
extraordinary
pair of glasses fitted
beneath a hat. With such
a contraption, the wearer
would raise a few
eyebrows today.
This rare pair is part
of the Essilor-Pierre Marly
collection (see page 196).*

The ultimate
accessory for an
outing to the theater.
This tortoiseshell curio has a
lorgnette and handle that doubles as
an ear trumpet and case to fold away the
fan. Fans with lorgnettes, or lorgnettes with
ear trumpets, were common. All three
functions, incorporated into the same item,
make this piece particularly rare.

In principle, these lorgnettes
are similar to those in the antique
eyeglasses section. What is unusual
about them is their handles which
have the same shape as their
frames; no attempt has been
made to conceal their functionality.

The lorgnette on the opposite
page is made of silver and
dates from the nineteenth
century. This one is made of dark
horn and dates from the same era.
The small elegant spur adorning
the right-hand rim is functional
as well as ornamental.
When folded, it enables
the frames to be clipped
into their case using
the hook at the bottom.

*The case of this beautifully crafted tortoiseshell
lorgnette from around 1880 also has the same shape
as its frames. Such original and well-made items
are tricky to find, especially in good condition.
Antique dealers can help you in your quest. In Paris,
Ghislaine Chaplier runs a delightful boutique,
and is always willing to help (see page 372).*

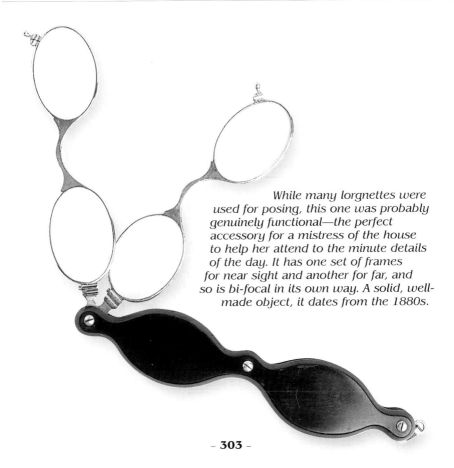

While many lorgnettes were used for posing, this one was probably genuinely functional—the perfect accessory for a mistress of the house to help her attend to the minute details of the day. It has one set of frames for near sight and another for far, and so is bi-focal in its own way. A solid, well-made object, it dates from the 1880s.

This lorgnette from the end of the
nineteenth century is fitted with
a watch, which, in itself, does not make
it a curio. However, its position, at the
far end of the handle, is unusual. In general,
the face and mechanism are encased
in the middle of the handle and fitted with
a cap to protect against possible knocks.

The heavy enameled handle, which doubles as a telescope, makes this lorgnette slightly unwieldy. This pair must be a desk model. The absence of any ring to affix it to a chain would confirm this theory.

With its attractive appliqué
decoration, this is a steel
lorgnette impersonating
a pair of binoculars. Its touch
of humor as well as the
quality of its craftsmanship
makes this 1880s model
most endearing.

*This model
has everything
a standard lorgnette needs—
a tortoiseshell handle
and frames, a magnifying lens,
and a ring for attachment
to a belt. But it only has one
eyepiece. Did it also have
a one-eyed owner?*

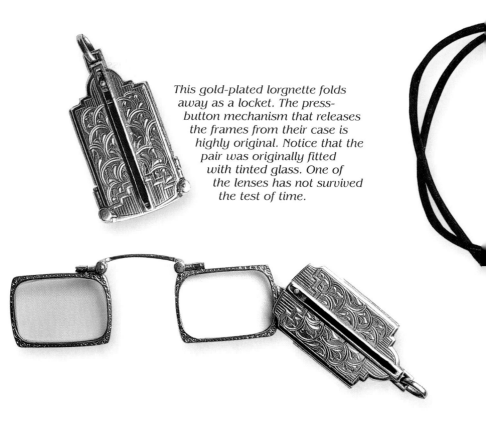

This gold-plated lorgnette folds away as a locket. The press-button mechanism that releases the frames from their case is highly original. Notice that the pair was originally fitted with tinted glass. One of the lenses has not survived the test of time.

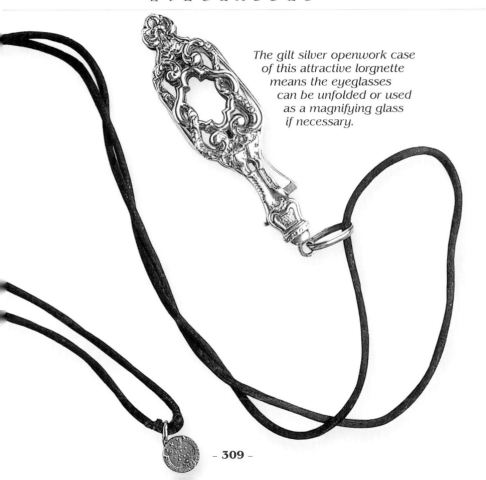

*The gilt silver openwork case
of this attractive lorgnette
means the eyeglasses
can be unfolded or used
as a magnifying glass
if necessary.*

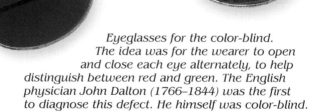

*Eyeglasses for the color-blind.
The idea was for the wearer to open
and close each eye alternately, to help
distinguish between red and green. The English
physician John Dalton (1766–1844) was the first
to diagnose this defect. He himself was color-blind.*

Separate red and blue lenses
can, in certain cases, prove
to be useful. The effect that
superimposing red on blue might have,
however, is unclear, unless this pair were
actually made for someone with a penchant for the
color combination. Color perception problems come
in very different forms depending on the person.

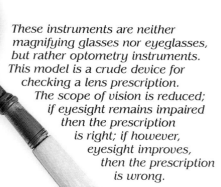

These instruments are neither
magnifying glasses nor eyeglasses,
but rather optometry instruments.
This model is a crude device for
checking a lens prescription.
The scope of vision is reduced;
if eyesight remains impaired
then the prescription
is right; if however,
eyesight improves,
then the prescription
is wrong.

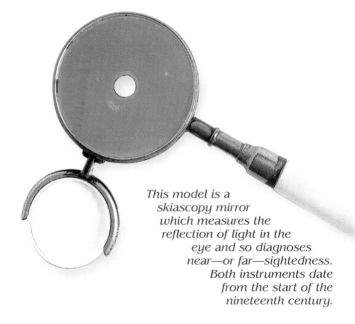

This model is a skiascopy mirror which measures the reflection of light in the eye and so diagnoses near—or far—sightedness. Both instruments date from the start of the nineteenth century.

This lorgnette, with its multiple frames, was not for home use. These are test lenses, once used by opticians, to select the most suitable strength for their clients. Until the 1930s, most eyeglasses were sold ready-mounted with lenses that offered only standard correction.

Another set of optician's test lenses. These are in tortoiseshell and were used to make eye tests more precise. In the same vein, there are also gauges for clients to test the different possible tints of their lenses.

This is an ingenious little magnifying glass that can be used without even being unfolded. The wearer simply looks through the hole in the middle of the handle-case. When deployed, the frame offers a wider field of vision.

*Some claim that this type of glasses, with their fine
wire-mesh side-shields, was used by locomotive
drivers to protect their eyes from soot. A train
specialist we have consulted rejects this idea ...*

*... and believes
that such eyewear
was actually worn
by laborers operating
grinders or lathes.*

The idea of workplace safety has developed greatly
in the last fifty years, though there has always been
some notion of its importance. In the 1920s,
for example, a number of catalogues issued
by eyeglasses manufacturers targeted "aviators,
drivers, motorcyclists, and workshops."
They offered a range of "protective" models
but gave no specific indication of their use.

This pair might have
been used by wood,
iron, and stone workers or
welders for eye protection.
Some cycling glasses very
much resemble this design.

This pair has a clear purpose,
for locomotive operation (one has lost
its elastic). Their original red metal box
supplied by the French state railway corporation
means they can be identified with precision.

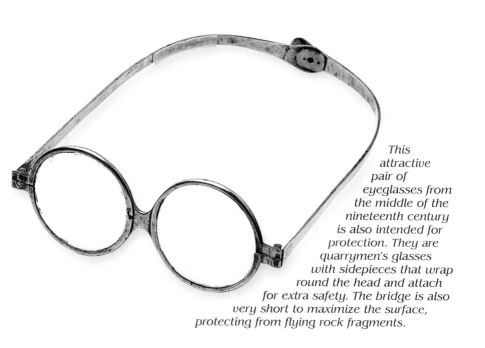

This attractive pair of eyeglasses from the middle of the nineteenth century is also intended for protection. They are quarrymen's glasses with sidepieces that wrap round the head and attach for extra safety. The bridge is also very short to maximize the surface, protecting from flying rock fragments.

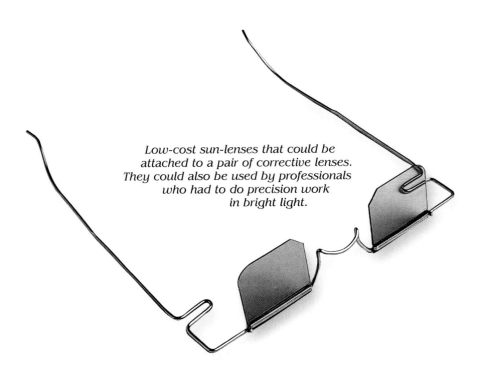

Low-cost sun-lenses that could be
attached to a pair of corrective lenses.
They could also be used by professionals
who had to do precision work
in bright light.

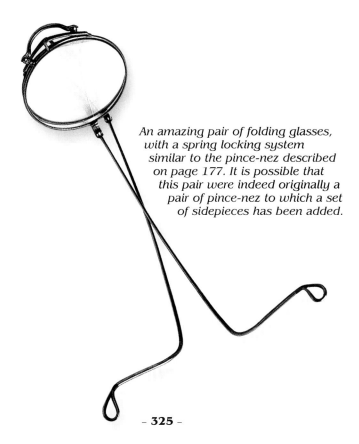

An amazing pair of folding glasses, with a spring locking system similar to the pince-nez described on page 177. It is possible that this pair were indeed originally a pair of pince-nez to which a set of sidepieces has been added.

This unusually shaped pince-nez was not produced by a manufacturer with a sense of humor; it was actually patented in 1950 by the optician Loker, enabling near— and far—sight according to the same principle as half-moon lenses.

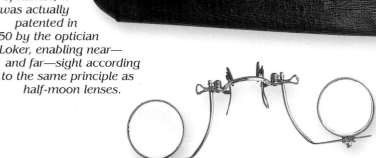

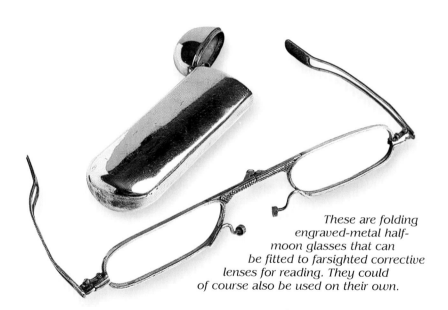

These are folding engraved-metal half-moon glasses that can be fitted to farsighted corrective lenses for reading. They could of course also be used on their own.

LOUPE BINOCULAIRE RÉGLABLE

BREVETÉE FRANCE & ÉTRANGER

Le dispositif de cet appareil permet la vision des deux yeux ensemble, avec écartement pupillaire approprié à chaque personne. — Donne plusieurs grossissements.

Seule Loupe
permettant
la vision en relief
sans
déformation
des images
et sans fatigue

Vision des deux
yeux par la
mise au point
des
centres optiques
la fusion se fait
normalement

APPAREIL MUNI DE LENTILLES Nº I

Cet appareil a l'avantage de laisser les deux mains libres, de conserver devant les yeux lunette ou pince-nez, de voir autour de soi sans la moindre gêne. Rend les plus grands services au Monde Médical Dentaire et Chimiste, dans les laboratoires, aux Dessinateurs, Graveurs, Lithographes, Horlogers, Photographes retoucheurs, etc., etc...

It is rare for optical devices to still have their accompanying packaging. "This device enables use of both eyes at once. The lens position may be adjusted. Several enlargement sizes available." The fine print on the bottom of the box reads: "The advantages of this device are that it leaves both hands free. The wearer need not remove his glasses or pince-nez and so can look around unimpeded. The spectacles render the greatest of services to the domains of medicine, dentistry, and science, and to laboratory workers, illustrators, engravers, lithographers, clock makers, and photographers, etc., etc.."

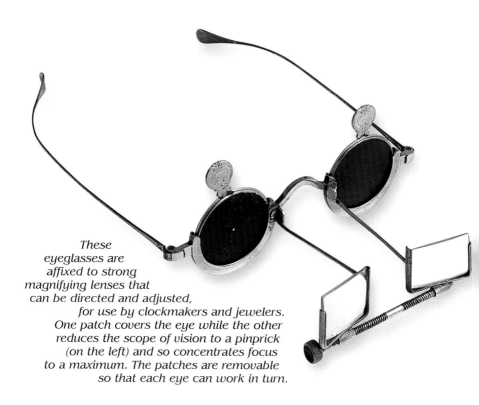

*These
eyeglasses are
affixed to strong
magnifying lenses that
can be directed and adjusted,
for use by clockmakers and jewelers.
One patch covers the eye while the other
reduces the scope of vision to a pinprick
(on the left) and so concentrates focus
to a maximum. The patches are removable
so that each eye can work in turn.*

*This amazing pair were dubbed "bed spectacles"
by their manufacturer as they dispense with the need
to hold one's reading material right in front of the
face—a tiring activity at the best of times.
The weary reader need only prop the book on his
or her chest and a rectifying prism directs the image
of the text back to the eyes.*

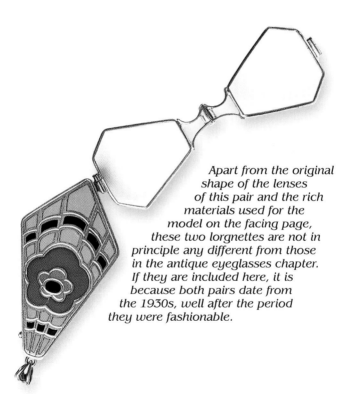

Apart from the original
shape of the lenses
of this pair and the rich
materials used for the
model on the facing page,
these two lorgnettes are not in
principle any different from those
in the antique eyeglasses chapter.
If they are included here, it is
because both pairs date from
the 1930s, well after the period
they were fashionable.

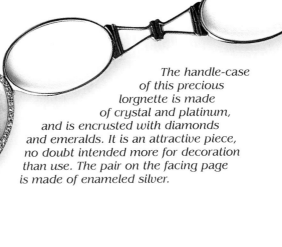

The handle-case
of this precious
lorgnette is made
of crystal and platinum,
and is encrusted with diamonds
and emeralds. It is an attractive piece,
no doubt intended more for decoration
than use. The pair on the facing page
is made of enameled silver.

This folding model
from the 1950s is quite hilarious.
It seems to be made of Bakelite,
engraved and encrusted with paste
jewels. Lorgnettes can be extremely
varied ...

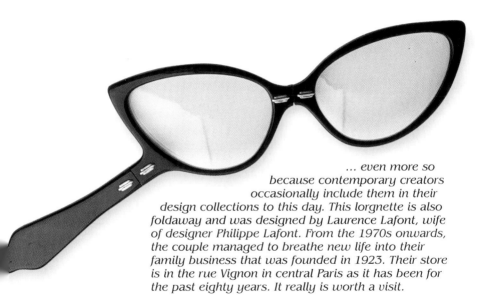

... even more so
because contemporary creators
occasionally include them in their
design collections to this day. This lorgnette is also
foldaway and was designed by Laurence Lafont, wife
of designer Philippe Lafont. From the 1970s onwards,
the couple managed to breathe new life into their
family business that was founded in 1923. Their store
is in the rue Vignon in central Paris as it has been for
the past eighty years. It really is worth a visit.

*Do not be
mistaken. These pairs
are not the creation of a young
designer working on a science fiction movie.
They are in fact almost a hundred years old
and were worn by native Inuit.*

*They are
obviously of local manufacture and
cleverly protect against both the sun and the wind
but also against the reflection of the sun
on the snow. Another important feature
is that they never fog up.*

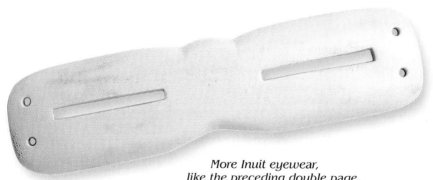

More Inuit eyewear,
like the preceding double page,
made of wood, horn or bone, as in this case,
sometimes decorated in geometrical shapes.
Such pairs were tied around the head by string,
ribbon, or even rubber.

*If "necessity is the mother of invention," invention is the
mother of design. These are not modern Inuit shades
but a model created for the fashion house Courrèges,
designed by the optician Pierre Marly. This model was
a part of Pierre Marly's own personal collection, which
was recently acquired by Essilor (see page 197).*

If the millions of modern
creations are an eyesore
to you, why not take
an old pair of frames
and fit corrective
lenses adapted to your
needs. Marc Chaplier,
an antiques dealer,
specializing in, among
other things, eyewear
from the past
(see addresses
page 372), did
exactly that with
this pair of
attractive folding
eyeglasses in
tortoiseshell and silver
dating from the 1930s.

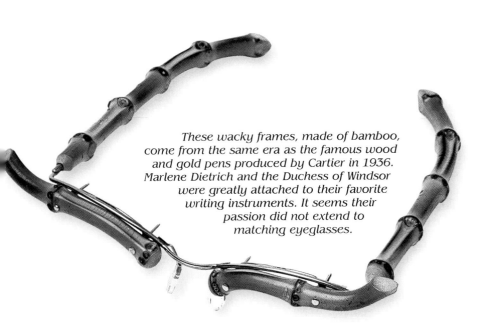

These wacky frames, made of bamboo,
come from the same era as the famous wood
and gold pens produced by Cartier in 1936.
Marlene Dietrich and the Duchess of Windsor
were greatly attached to their favorite
writing instruments. It seems their
passion did not extend to
matching eyeglasses.

Folding glasses from the 1970s. Their sidepieces are similar to old-style temple glasses (see page 59). One of their sales pitches was that they could be worn by women at the hairdresser without hindering delicate scissor work. This, it appears, was not reason enough to guarantee success.

This pair, with their hinged bridge, was supposed to be adaptable to all face shapes. The problem is that the hinge is so big that, unless the wearer has a large nose, they have to be folded at quite an angle to fit. This forces the sidepieces downwards, which is uncomfortable for the ears.

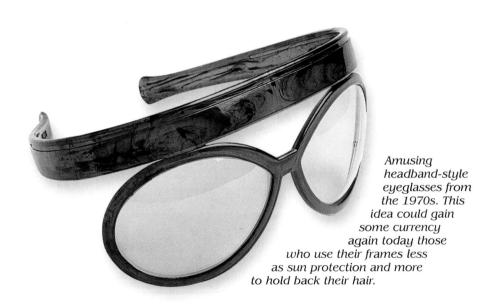

*Amusing
headband-style
eyeglasses from
the 1970s. This
idea could gain
some currency
again today those
who use their frames less
as sun protection and more
to hold back their hair.*

*Another
idea that could
be recycled in these
ecological times is
wooden glasses. The disadvantage is that
the material is fairly heavy in comparison to the feather-light
metals and plastics to which we have grown accustomed.*

A quality pair of glasses is never made of a single
material. A plastic model will always be fitted
with metal hinges and screws. Sometimes the frames
are fitted with metal tenons that connect
the sidepieces to the rim while sometimes
the sidepieces are reinforced by metal inserts.

Similarly, as is plain to see on this striking, recent creation, metal glasses nearly always have plastic parts, in this case, the sleeves on each sidepiece and the nose pads.

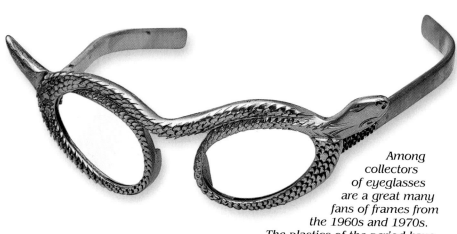

Among
collectors
of eyeglasses
are a great many
fans of frames from
the 1960s and 1970s.
The plastics of the period have
not always survived the test of time and little can be
done to restore them. There are certain precautions that
can be taken, however. You should store eyeglasses
of different materials separately as some plastics
decompose in contact with others.

*Like its neighbor, this pair of glasses dates
from the 1970s. It is, not surprisingly, American-made,
created by the Anglo-American brand, Eyewear.
The monuments on this model could be adaptable
according to the city or country.*

AMAZING

*A cute pair, decorated with doves, called Birds,
and another, facing page, dubbed Swans,
to suit the mood you are in. These two pairs
of eyeglasses were produced by Anglo-American
Optical. If originality is your cup of tea ...*

*... then try seeking out a rare pair of glasses
made for cats and dogs or the small eyepieces
used to obstruct the view of roosters
and pheasants to stop them fighting.*

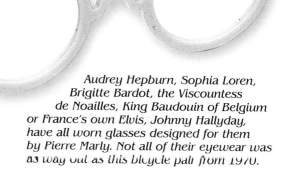

*Audrey Hepburn, Sophia Loren,
Brigitte Bardot, the Viscountess
de Noailles, King Baudouin of Belgium
or France's own Elvis, Johnny Hallyday,
have all worn glasses designed for them
by Pierre Marly. Not all of their eyewear was
as way out as this bicycle pair from 1970.*

*Here is the
modern day equivalent
of the binocular-shaped
lorgnette on page 306.*

This pair may seem standard, but, on closer inspection, you will notice their sidepieces in the shape of forks. The long sleeves enhance the trompe-l'oeil effect. The model was designed by Jean-Paul Gaultier.

*This pair of hands, with their imitation
precious stone nails, clasps the head in a slightly
worrying way. Humor is not the preserve
of renowned designers: this pair, from the US,
has no brand name.*

Alain Mikli states that the glasses he designs are "just as much for seeing as being seen." With models such as these, we can take him at his word. He created his brand back in 1978, at the age of 23, when the ink on his optician's diploma was not yet dry.

Today, Alain Mikli sells more than 500,000 pairs every year around the world. This is proof enough that in our age, eyewear eccentricity is not only tolerated but much sought after.

*Stars and celebrities worldwide have worn Alain Mikli
frames. One of the first to wear a pair on stage
was none other than Elton John, in 1983. It remains
to be seen how tomorrow's collectors will react
when they find a pair like these. Will they feel the same
emotion as when in the presence of a pair
of seventeenth century spectacles?*

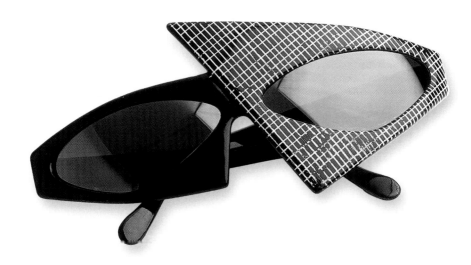

This photograph is not a reduction. These are miniature pairs of glasses for dolls with real lenses and metal hinges. Just like grown-up spectacles!

*Here is an antique version of glasses
to observe eclipses, and facing is
a model produced for the total
solar eclipse of August 11, 1999.
They might only have been worn
for an hour but they are nevertheless
historical eyeglasses with
which many of us
are familiar.*

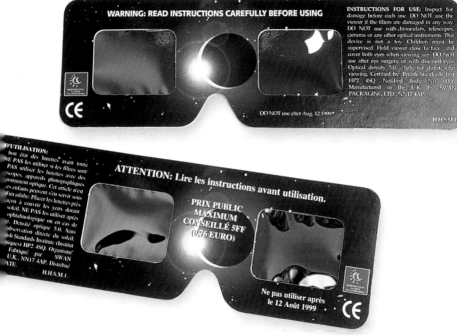

WARNING: READ INSTRUCTIONS CAREFULLY BEFORE USING

INSTRUCTIONS FOR USE: Inspect for damage before each use. DO NOT use the viewer if the filters are damaged in any way. DO NOT use with binoculars, telescopes, cameras or any other optical instruments. This device is not a toy. Children must be supervised. Hold viewer close to face and cover both eyes when viewing sun. DO NOT use after eye surgery, or with diseased eyes. Optical density 5.0 - Safe for direct solar viewing. Certified by British Standards Inst. HP2 4SQ. Notified Body No. 0086. Manufactured in the U.K. by SWAN PACKAGING LTD., NN17 4AP.

DO NOT use after Aug. 12 1999

HHSM1

D'UTILISATION: bon état des lunettes avant toute NE PAS les utiliser si les filtres sont PAS utiliser les lunettes avec des scopes, appareils photographiques instrument optique. Cet article n'est es enfants peuvent s'en servir sous d'un adulte. Placer les lunettes près açon à couvrir les yeux durant soleil. NE PAS les utiliser après ophtalmologique ou en cas de Densité optique 5.0. Sans observation directe du soleil. sh Standards Institute (Institut iques) HP2 4SQ. Organisme Fabriqué par SWAN U.K. NN17 4AP. Distribué ATE. H.H.S.M.I.

ATTENTION: Lire les instructions avant utilisation.

PRIX PUBLIC MAXIMUM CONSEILLÉ 5FF (0,76 EURO)

Ne pas utiliser après le 12 Août 1999

*These objects
are definitely not
eyeglasses—they're ashtrays.
The cat logo is a familiar feature in Morez,
where it is displayed in neon. It is the emblem
of the Marius Morel workshop,
which was founded in 1880 ...*

... *by Jules Morel, then*
developed by his son Marius.
Today the brand is sold around
the world. The ashtray on this page
has Archives Optique written on its base
and was produced by a Parisian optician.

As a rule, all collectors,
however serious they are,
will never let a gimmick
related to their
predilection pass
them by. There
are not many joke
eyeglasses around.
This example needs
little introduction.

*You can fit your favorite lenses
in here. Well, in photographic form
at least, as this is a photo frame.
The ideal gift for a proud collector
with pictures to prove it.*

Index,
Bibliography,
Acknowledgments
and Addresses

Index

The index features the main proper names, place names, brand names, and models that appear throughout the text.

INDEX

AU PARADIS DES DAMES
8 & 10, RUE DE RIVOLI

Mon Jargonn

INDEX

The following is a list of eyeglasses and related objects from Essilor-Pierre's collection:
page 17, pages 22 and 23, page 25, page 26, page 28, page 35, page 39, pages 42–49,
pages 58–60, pages 62–65, pages 112 and 113, pages 117–121, pages 124–129,
page 142, pages 145 and 146, pages 158 and 159, page 163, pages 181–183,
pages 185–199, pages 201–209, pages 230–233, page 235, page 244, pages 246–256,
page 269, pages 296–297, page 304, page 311, page 323, pages 336–338,
pages 341 and 342, 345 and 346 and pages 348–353.

Bibliography

Bussod, Michel, and Michel Jean-Prost. *La Petite-Fille des Rivières, historique de la lunetterie dans le canton de Morez.* La Biennoise, 1996.

Corson, Richard. *Fashions in Eyeglass.* London: Peter Owen, 1967.

Essilor 1972–1997: Mieux voir le monde. Published to celebrate the 25th anniversary of Essilor, 1997.

Girard, Sylvie. *Les Lunettes, sept siècles pour mieux voir.* Brussels: Editions Casterman, 1991.

Marly, Pierre, Paul Biérent, and Jean-Claude Margolin. *Lunettes & lorgnettes.* Paris: Editions Hoëbeke, 1988.

Pascal, Dominique. *Objets de l'automobile à collectionner.* Editions MDM, 1998.

Vitols, Astrid. *Dictionnaire des lunettes, historique et symbolique d'un objet culturel.* Paris: Editions Bonneton, 1994.

Various antique catalogs from eyeglass manufacturers and distributors were also used.

Acknowledgments and Addresses

*This book could not have been written and illustrated
without the valuable assistance and availability of the following people,
whom I thank from the bottom of my heart.*

*– Anne-Marie Melin, wife of Jean Melin, who, despite
the sad death of her husband, welcomed us with immense kindness
and generosity. I would hope that the many items from his collection
illustrated in these pages provide a fitting homage to the memory
of a man who was passionate about eyeglasses. He loved them
for their intrinsic beauty, for their ingenuity, and for their diversity
of forms and their materials. A true collector.*

*– Marc and Ghislaine Chaplier, antique dealers specializing
in small, collectible quality items, including optics.
They were very generous with their time, and their passion
for beautiful objects is contagious.*
Ghislaine Chaplier
Village Suisse, galerie n° 65
10, avenue de Champaubert
75015 Paris, France
Tel and fax: 33 (0)1 45 67 30 55
E-mail: galeriechaplier@aol.com
Website: www.ghislainechaplier.com

– At Essilor International, the CEO Philippe Alfroid and legal expert
Ghislaine Oger, as well as Nathalie Schwartz, head of interdepartmental
communication, followed the progress of this book and guided me very
efficiently through the many pieces of the Essilor-Pierre Marly collection.

Essilor
147, rue de Paris
94227 Charenton Cedex, France
Tel: 33 (0)1 49 77 42 24 - Fax: 33 (0)1 49 77 45 30

– Bernard Maitenaz, former CEO of Essilor,
for his careful rereading and technical advice.

– Thyphaine Le Foll, curator of the Morez Eyeglasses Museum,
for the help and time she gave.

Musée de la Lunette
Place Jean-Jaurès
39400 Morez, France
Tel: 33 (0)3 84 33 39 30 - Fax: 33 (0)3 84 33 26 42
E-mail: musee-de-la-lunette@mairie-morez.fr
Website: www.haut-jura.com

– Jean-Manuel Finot, CEO of E.B. Meyrowitz, for his warm welcome and
invaluable information about brand names. The majority of models
featured in the sports glasses section were photographed in his store.

Meyrowitz
5, rue de Castiglione
75001 Paris, France
Tel: 33 (0)1 42 60 63 64 - Fax: 33 (0)1 42 61 36 30
E-mail: meyrowitz@meyrowitz.com
Website: www.meyrowitz.com

There are also two Meyrowitz stores in London:
6, The Royal Arcade
28 Old Bond Street
London WIX 3HD, United Kingdom
Tel: 44 (0)20 74935778

79, Elizabeth Street - Belgravia
London SWI W9PJ, United Kingdom
Tel: 44 (0)20 77300202
E-mail: ebmeyrowitz@aol.com

– Thank you also to Christian Receveur, CEO of the Forsym
group and head of the Lunetiers du Jura, the employers'
association for the eyewear profession.
Website: www.lunetiers-du-jura.com

– And thank you to Agnès Bonnaventure-Récolet,
head of communication with the L' Amy group.
L' Amy
216, rue de la République
39401 Morez Cedex, France
Tel: 33 (0)3 84 33 77 00 - Fax: 33 (0)3 84 33 76 69
Website: www.lamygroup.com

There is an attractive eyeglass museum in Italy:
Museo dell'Occhiale
39, via degli Alpini
32044 Pieve di Cadore, Italy
Tel: 39 043 5500294
Website: www.sunrise.it/musei/occhiale

In the same collection

Collectible Hand Tools
by Dominique Pascal
ISBN: 2-0803-0438-0

Collectible Wristwatches
by René Pannier
ISBN: 2-0801-0621-X

Collectible Pipes
by Jean Rebeyrolles
ISBN: 2-0801-0884-0

Collectible Lighters
by Juan Manuel Clark
ISBN: 2-0801-1133-7

Collectible Pocket Knives
by Dominique Pascal
ISBN: 2-0801-0550-7

Collectible Corkscrews
by Frédérique Crestin–Billet
ISBN: 2-0801-0551-5

Collectible Miniature Perfume Bottles
by Anne Breton
ISBN: 2-0801-0632-5

Collectible Fountain Pens
by Juan Manuel Clark
ISBN: 2-0801-0719-4

Collectible Miniature Cars
by Dominique Pascal
ISBN: 2-0801-0718-6

Collectible Model Trains
by David-Paul Gurney
ISBN: 2-081-1142-6

Collectible Snowdomes
by Lélie Carnot
ISBN: 2-0801-0889-1

Collectible Playing Cards
by Frédérique Crestin-Billet
ISBN: 2-0801-1134-5

Collectible Toy Soldiers
by Dominique Pascal
ISBN: 2-0801-1141-8

Collectible
HAND TOOLS
Dominique Pascal

Flammarion

Collectible
WRISTWATCHES
René Pannier

Flammarion

Collectible
PIPES
Jean Rebeyrolles

Flammarion

Collectible
LIGHTERS

Juan Manuel Clarke

Flammarion

Collectible
POCKET
KNIVES

Dominique Pascal

Flammarion

Collectible
CORKSCREWS

Frédérique Crestin-Billet

Flammarion

Collectible
MODEL
TRAINS
David-Paul Gurney

Flammarion

Collectible
SNOWDOMES
Leslie Carnot

Flammarion

Collectible
PLAYING CARDS
Frédérique Crestin-Billet

Flammarion

Collectible
TOY
SOLDIERS
Dominique Pascal

Flammarion

Photographic Credits

With the exception of the illustrations on pages 22–23, 39,
and 142, which are from the Essilor archives,
all color photos were produced by Antoine Pascal and Dominique Pascal
and come from Archives & Collections.
E–mail: archives.collections@wanadoo.fr
All rights reserved for other documents.

418758